South Croxton

...the village on the hill

Philip Snelders

South Croxton

ISBN 978-0-9550245-1-1

Published by South Croxton Parish Council and Glin Press, 5, Leicester St., Melton Mowbray LE13 0PP
Printed and bound by Chartwell Press, 171, Waterside Rd., Hamilton, Leicester LE5 1TL

The Village Archive, consisting of nearly seven hundred photographs, maps, documents, newspaper articles and video clips, as well as of the present houses in the village, are on a CDRom. It can be purchased for £10.00, plus 75p.postage where required. Orders to P.Snelders, 85. Main St., South Croxton, LE7 3RL (e-mail philsnel@aol.com).

Profits from this book and the CDRom will be divided equally between the Church and the Village Hall.

First Edition 2007
Second Edition 2008

To Lesley, my anchor, who, when I get too involved with the past, reminds me that there is a present and a future.

Foreword

In 1994 I thought it would be fun to ask for old photographs of South Croxton and display them in the Church at the Arts Festival in 1996. I expected a dozen or two. There were 80. This was the start of the Village Archive, because the bug hit me and I began collecting photographs, quotations, articles, and documents of all sorts about the village. I was anxious to get the originals back to their owners, so I took many into town and had them copied by laser - few of us had heard of scanners and digital cameras in those days. SCAF (South Croxton Arts Festival) gave me a small grant to enable me to do this. It all just grew, and this booklet is one of the results. It should be particularly noted that I am not an historian, nor an archivist - but someone had to do it.

I am most grateful to the many people who have helped me with this and other projects concerning the village, especially those who lent me photographs. In particular I am indebted to Freda Elliott, backed by her brother, Fred Draycott, who has not only contributed to the book and was part of every group conversation about the village, but also read and commented on several bits of the book. I am also indebted to the work done by the Historical Society in the late 1970s under Roy King, whose typed notes have been very helpful. Particular thanks also go to Vanessa McLoughlin and Dr.Graham Jones of The Local History Department of Leicester University, and Richard Knox of the Leicestershire County Council Archaeology Team. I am also indebted to Julian Duxbury for his interest and encouragement, his contributions and additional research, and assistance in getting the book published; to Nigel Bannister for the 'electronic typesetting'; and to Bill Langley for printing it at his Chartwell Press. It should be noted that all the last three live in the village, so this is truly a village enterprise.

I hope that the publication of this booklet will prompt its readers to correct the text, to add to it, to produce more photographs, to add to the store of memories about the village. Any such contributions will be gratefully received and recorded. I acknowledge that all mistakes and inaccuracies are mine, despite the help given to me by so many.

Philip Snelders
South Croxton 2005

Acknowledgements

I am very grateful for the following who have agreed to allow me to incorporate their work into this book:

B.J.Craven of 'Pondlife Creative' for the cover and title page illustration,
6. East Ave. Syston, Leicester LE7 2EH Tel:0771 573 4458

Village photograph © Kate Jewell 2005, use licensed under a Creative Commons Licence

R.N.Trubshaw for photographs of the Church and gargoyles marked (BT), and information on the gargoyles, and the Moody Bush Stone, www.hoap.com 2, Cross Hill Close, Wymeswold, Loughborough LE126UJ

Olwyn Hughes of the Leicester Mercury for permission to reproduce her sketch of the village

Chartwell Press for their help with the book.

Other acknowledgements appear in the text.

This book was finished in October 2005. Applications then went off to eight charities for a grant to help with the printing of the book. Each of them replied charmingly, said that the giving of a grant for this purpose was not within their remit, and suggested other places we might try. We finally went to Awards for All, and they spent a long time getting more information from us to get the application just right, before finally refusing on the grounds that we did not fulfil the aims of the grant. In all cases we would have been on firmer ground if we had wanted to open a Youth Club, but the printing of a book fell firmly between their various stools.

However, something good has come out of it. In the intervening period digital printing has been introduced, which means that the books can be produced more cheaply, they can be changed more readily, and the illustrations can be distributed throughout the book, as was originally intended. The author and publishers are very grateful to the printers, Chartwell Press, of whom Bill Langley is the owner, for printing the book at cost, and for accepting the money we had collected as an advance payment, and then offering to wait for the sale of books to pay the remainder of the cost.

The Index has been almost hand done, so I am responsible and apologise for mistakes that occur there.

Philip Snelders
South Croxton 2007

viii South Croxton

Aerial view

Contents

Village view downhill

1 History of the Village of South Croxton

Village circa 1960

The present village

South Croxton is a small, rural, conservation village 8 miles to the north east of Leicester, and between Scraptoft and Melton Mowbray. It lies on the southern slope of a hill, and on the 400ft.(122m.) contour at the top of the hill. The geology is boulder clay with pockets of glacial sand and gravel. At the top of the hill is the Church of St.John the Baptist and a medieval moated site. It has currently (2005) 90 houses, and there were 234 persons at the time of the last census in 2001. It has three farms (in 1951 there were 10 within the village boundary(1) and a pub. The Post Office/shop closed in 1988, although the Post Office has since been located in the pub and in houses, and was open two mornings a week. That arrangement has now ceased. There is a very lively community spirit in the village, and events like walks, a bonfire on November 5th, dances and Family Fun Days are held regularly. The Village Hall, formerly the school, is in use for regular meetings of the Village Hall Committee and the Parish Council, for birthday parties, travelling entertainment and other special events. Of special note was the South Croxton Arts Festival which was held every two years from 1974 until 2002. It was originally an exhibition of art in the Village Hall with refreshments. It then grew in size and reputation, so that there were open gardens, musical events notably in the Church, and other entertainments, with over 3,000 visitors over the two days of the August Bank Holiday, preceded by a village dinner and dance in the marquee behind the Village Hall especially erected for the Festival. Weather prevented a successful festival in 2002, and as the Art organiser and originator, John Redfern, had retired from the festival in 2000, and the Chairman, Brian Piper, had resigned in 2002, the festival fell into abeyance. Every year a Vintage Working Weekend is held on local farmland.

Aspects of the village.

The best view of the village at a distance is from the Beeby Road, and from the Ridgemere. Entering the village from the Ridgemere, The Grange and South Manor Farm are on the left, and the first bend in the road comes immediately after that. A road bridge built in the fifties crosses the Queniborough Brook. Previous to that there was a ford with a footbridge next to it, some of which can still be seen down stream from the present bridge. From the brook the road continues straight until just after School Lane and Kings Lane when it starts meandering up the hill, and gets steeper. The hill is surmounted by North Manor Farm and the Church, with the mediaeval moated site beyond that. Most of the older houses are built with long fronts on the edge of the pavement, or set a little back. This gives a special character to the village, and gives a relatively intimate human scale, enclosed, as compared with the wide countryside around. It gives it a 'distinctive grain, scale and appearance', as a background paper for Charnwood Borough Council says. Interspersed with the older and the modern houses are the surviving houses from the late eighteenth and nineteenth centuries, and more distinguished houses from the late Georgian and early Victorian periods. School Lane was developed from the 1950s onwards, first with the building of council houses (of which only one remains in council hands). Five earlier buildings survive on School Lane, Sunny Dene, now called The Old School House, Barley Leys cottage, once a pair of cottages, now restored and modernised but still with two staircases, no.32, which has been extensively modernised, no.42, enlarged several times, and with substantial grounds and a lake, and nos.35 and 37, a pair of cottages. On Kings Lane there are only Fox Cottages, a pair of cottages built in the 18th.century for workers on the Baggrave estate, and modernised. The pavements and kerbs are modern, except for some surviving granite kerbs alongside North Manor Farm, Hill Top Farm, Maida Vale at the corner of School Lane, and a few kerb stones on the corner of Kings Lane outside the Golden Fleece. There are four listed buildings in the village - the Church (Grade II*, a particularly important building of more than special interest), North Manor Farm (Grade II, a building of special interest warranting every effort to preserve it) parts of which date from the 17th.century, Hill Top Farm (Grade II), and South Manor Farm (Grade II). The buildings put up in the second half of the last century, mainly the ribbon development along Kings Lane and School Lane, have in general not respected the form or materials of the older buildings, but have been built according to the taste of their several ages, and will become the historical buildings of the future. The most extensive views from the village, often across rooftops and between buildings, are to the south and east, coming downhill, and overlooking the brook.

<u>Origins of the village</u>

The history of the village goes back into antiquity. In Saxon times and before it would have been a good spot for a settlement, on the top of a hill with springs available. How far back it was established is not known. Bronze Age (2,000-750B.C.) artefacts have been found nearby along the Ridgemere, in Queniborough and in the village(2). At the excavation of the moated site (see chapter on 'Archaeology') artefacts dating from 850 A.D. were found. Among them were a Saxon pin, some 9th century pottery, a silver penny of Aethelread II (978-1016A.D.), as well as material from later dates. The Saxon origin of at least part of the village is indicated both by the name, and by the phrase in Domesday - 'Godric held it', indicating the ownership by a person with a Saxon name prior to the Conquest. So the pre-Conquest origin of the settlement is clear.

Syston's foundation would not have been before 500. Later some Saxons who settled there would have followed the track along the higher ridge (Ridgemere), particularly if it had been trodden out by the Celts, until they arrived at another good place for a settlement. They would have found the springs at the top of the hill, perhaps previously used by the Celts. They would have cleared the woodland downhill to, and perhaps past the brook, built their wattle and daub, thatched homes, some near the top of the hill, and some nearer the brook, and sown crops. Gradually, a few other buildings would have been built between the two, a roadway passing the houses in Saxon style down the hill, and a thriving community established. This is quite a likely story, which fits the known facts.

The Village Name

In this immediate area villages' names end mainly in '-ton' and '-ham' which indicate an early, Saxon origin, or '-by' and '- thorpe' which indicate a later Viking origin. (These Vikings were originally from Denmark. The Norwegian Vikings went to Shetland, the Orkneys, and from there to Ireland.) There are very few village names of Viking origin beyond the A46 (the old Roman Fosse Way linking Cirencester and Lincoln) and the Wreake River. These seemed to be barrier beyond which the Vikings did not venture much. Indeed, the Wreake formed a natural barrier, and there is a high concentration of Viking villages along its banks, along the A607. The village was within the Danelaw, the area controlled by the Vikings from 878A.D.

At various times in the past the village has been called 'Crochestone' (Domesday), Croptone (Domesday), Crofon (the 'f' is a form of 's'), Crokeftune, Crowson, and Crowfston juxta (near) Baggrave. The name is pronounced by locals 'Crowson' to this day. The earliest mention of 'South' Croxton (Suð Croxton) is to be found in a document of 1204. It has also been known as Suð Crowston, and Suth-croxton. 'Croxton' is not an uncommon village name. There are a number of Croxtons in England, two in Staffordshire, two in Norfolk, one in Cambridgeshire, one in Humberside, Croxton Green in Cheshire, and Croxton Kerrial in Leicestershire. One view is that Croxton is a variant on the Latin for 'cross' (Latin - 'crux'), and perhaps refers to the Preaching Cross that once stood here. It is held by others that the name derives from an Old Viking name, Kruc, meaning crook backed, or 'crooked', plus 'tun' Saxon for homestead or village. Indeed, instead of being straight, the main road has at least two turns in it, and is crooked. However, it is equally likely that the origin of the name is Saxon, from 'croc', meaning a corner of land, or a name, 'Croc'. There are two other reasons to suppose that its origin is Saxon rather than Danish. First, the shape of the village is typically Saxon - a long street with houses on both sides, and rear plots backing onto the surrounding fields, a pattern which the present farms follow around the village. Second, the churchyard is typically Saxon, that is, on the top of a hill, and raised.

The epithet 'South' is more problematic. There is no 'North' Croxton, for example. There are a number of villages with the prefix 'South' to which there is no corresponding 'North', for example South Alkham in Kent or South Weston in Oxfordshire. One explanation might be that the village was originally beyond the church, but developed to the south of the church. It is curious that the church is not at the very apex of the hill; the road rises after the Church. The moated site is at the apex, and there is evidence of some settlement beyond the church, because at the time of the excavation around the moat several house platforms were noted. It was sometimes the case that when plague or pestilence struck, the original village was abandoned and another settlement established nearby. In this case it would have been on the southern, warmer slope below the church, and it might then have been called 'South Croxton', because it lay south of the original village. There is no direct evidence of resettlement, however, in this case. W.G.Hoskins said in the 1970 Shell guide to Leicestershire that there were, "...considerable traces of the old village site to the north west of the church", although the dig of the moated site in 1972 did not find them, only a single building that was replaced on two occasions over time. Another view, the most probable, is that the village lay south of Croxton Kerrial, where there was an Abbey, founded in 1162, which for a time held the 'advowson', the right to appoint the priest in South Croxton. So in all probability South Croxton was so named to distinguish it from the other Croxton to the North, which then had added to it a personal name, ' Kerrial' in the middle of the 13th.century after Nicholas de Kyriel.

The Saxons started coming to this country peacefully in about 250A.D. They came in increasing numbers when the Romans finally left In 409A.D. They assimilated themselves over time with the original Celts, and an Anglo-Saxon culture emerged from a fusion of the two. This is one theory. Another is that the Saxons pushed the Celts before them to the Welsh border. This theory has received an impetus from recent DNA evidence taken from populations on either side of Offa's Dyke, built to keep the Celts in Wales. The village probably originated at some time in the latter half of the first millennium, when it was named.

Part of the village, beyond the former school in School Lane, and separated from the village by open ground, used to be known as 'Westhorpe' (or possibly Westthorpe) indicating a Viking influence. 'thorp(e)' is a Viking word, and one of its meanings is an outlying hamlet, or an area developed on the edge of a main village. Within the Danelaw, the lower boundary of which stretched from the Thames, up through the middle of England and ending on the north west coast, Leicester was one of the 'Five Boroughs' of middle England in which the Vikings established their military and administrative headquarters. South Croxton was therefore firmly within the Danelaw But if the village were of Danish foundation there would be no need for a particular part to be specially given a Danish name.

From this it can be deduced that the village is of Saxon origin, probably well before 878AD. when the Danelaw was established, with a later Viking addition. So it would have been founded before 800A.D., probably long before, but how long is uncertain. It can be further deduced that the village ran down the slope from the church, at least by 870A.D. because Westhorpe is quite a way downhill.

First Mentions

As with most small villages, the first written evidence of its existence appears in the Domesday Record(3). Monks were sent by the King to every corner of England to record the ownership of land for tax purposes: King William just wanted to know how much tax could be gathered. As one observer of the survey noted: "*There was no single hide nor a yard of land, nor indeed one ox nor one cow nor one pig which was left out".* People compared it to the Last Judgement, or Doomsday, when everyone had to give a reckoning before God, so that was what it was called. The monks were given a strict brief, and they had only certain questions to ask: for example, "Is there a mill?" not, "Is there a mill outside the village that you use in conjunction with other villages?" And the peasants knew only what they knew. They had no maps; there was only hearsay, and certainly no carefully kept records. So it is not surprising, with the limitations on the questions and the possible vagueness and ambiguity of many answers, that the record is uncertain.

There are two entries concerning South Croxton in Domesday; taken together they are evidence of sound and solid farming in the village and its fields. The following are transcriptions from Domesday; the first is as near to the original script as possible with modern typeset. Both are preceded by a facsimile of the original Domesday script.. We can see clearly how the script has been written with a broad quill pen, with horizontal lines thin, and the vertical strokes broad.

It is interesting to note that in 1986 the BBC decided to compile a modern Domesday to celebrate 900 years since the original. Many individual children and schools were involved, and a great amount of work went on. £2.5 million was spent on getting the information onto two interactive multi-media discs. It lasted until the old Acorn Microcomputer was obsolete, and the discs could not be read. The original Domesday, written on vellum with a quill pen, with ink made of vegetable dye, is still readable, locked in a specially made chest in London's Public Record Office in Kew. The new version lasted 16 years. Fortunately, after three years' work, British and American teams have worked out new ways to access the material using software that emulates the obsolete Acorn Microcomputer system and the video discs. And we moderns think we're so clever.

<u>Land of the Bishop of Lincoln</u>

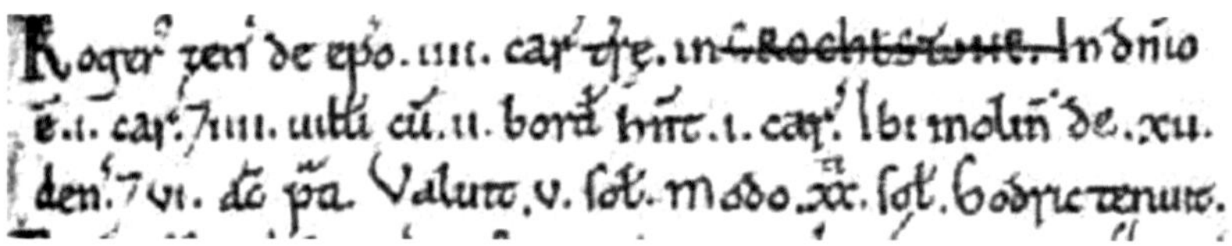

<u>Photocopy of Domesday 1086</u>

Roger ten. De epo.iiii.car trae,in *Crochestone.* In dnio
e.i.car.7 iiii.uitti.cu.ii.bord hnt.i.car.Ibi molin de.XII.
den.7 vi.ac pti.Valuit.v.fol.Modo.xx.fol.Godric tenuit.

Roger holds 4 c.of land in (South) Croxton from the Bishop.
In lordship 1 plough.
4 villagers with 2 smallholders have 1 plough.
A mill at 12d; meadow, 6 acres.

The value was 5s; now 20s.
Godric held it.

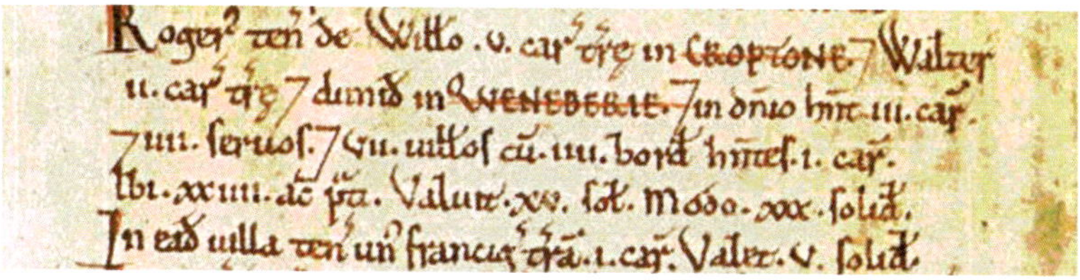

Scan from the Domesday Book 1086

Land of Robert of Tosne

Roger ten.de Witto.v.car trae in Croptone.7 Walter
II.car .trae in 7 dimid in Queneberie.7 in dnio hnt.iii.car.
7 IIII.feruos.7 vII.uittos cu.IIII.bord.hntes.1.car.
Ibi.xxIIII.ac pti.Valuit.xv.fol.Modo.xxx.foliđ.
In ead. villa ten un francig. Tra.1.car. Valet v. foliđ..

Robert holds 5carucates of land in (South) Croxton from William.
Walter (holds) 2½ carucates of land in Quenby. In Lordship they have
3 ploughs; 4 slaves.
7 villagers with 4 smallholders have 1 plough.
Meadow 2 acres.
The value was 15s; now 30s.
In the same village a Frenchman holds land for 1 plough.

(A carucate [*caruca*, Latin for a plough] is, in the Danelaw, a nominal 120 acres (490,000 m²), based on the area a plough team could till in a year. Outside the Danelaw the equivalent is a hide.)

It is likely that in pre-Conquest times the village had two foci, which later developed into two lordships, two manors, which is unusual in a village of its size. This was reflected in the two entries in the Domesday record, although whether they are about the two lordships is not absolutely certain.. This division can be traced through the Middle Ages, up to the 18th.century. The two Lordships were enclosed in the 18th.century at different times and in different ways. We still have today North Manor Farm and South Manor Farm.

Recent research has suggested that the land on the north side of the brook, belonging to the North Manor, might have been regarded as a unit with Barsby - see the chapter 'Recent Research'. And South Croxton seems to have been associated with a parcel of land on the brook that runs through Ashby. Could the mill have been there?

Further Records

In 1212 Sudcroxton is mentioned in the Coroners Rolls. In 1124-1129 there was a Leicestershire Survey, which also itemised the land and possessions of the county. This, like Domesday, is difficult to disentangle, because some of the land in South Croxton is credited to Quenby, for example, and there seem to be errors in the record

The only records of any activities after this are held in ecclesiastical records, and much of it is in the chapter on, and related to, the church.

Around 1227 King Henry III gave the manor (probably, but by no means certain, North Manor next to the church) to Henry de Burgh, his Chief Justice, who was also Earl of Kent. It is interesting to speculate that the village was known, or at least mentioned for a while in the highest quarters.

In 1297 Richard of Ashby was lord of the manor, and in 1346 his grandson was noted as 'lord of the village'. Between those dates the village changed dramatically, as both documentary and archaeological evidence show - see the chapter on 'Archaeology'.

Because of the kind of implements they used, the form of ploughing was 'ridge and furrow'. This feature abounds in fields in the area, which look corrugated, a result of this way of ploughing. The ploughs pushed out earth in only one direction, turning the soil towards the right hand side. They would go down one way, turn round, and come back again. Because of the small stature of their oxen it took eight to pull a plough, whereas five hundred years later it took only four. So at the end of their 'furrow long' (furlong) they would have had to swing before the end, giving the furrow a long 's' shape. Clusters of these furrows, pushing the earth towards the middle, would result in ridges a foot or so higher than the dip in between, which was also useful for drainage. These ridge and furrow fields can be seen fairly clearly on aerial photographs. The Saxons used every bit of land available to them. So if we look carefully at aerial photographs of the village we can see ridge and furrow fields on every side, pressing in on the boundaries of the village. Where they ended would be the mediaeval outline of the village, and this has been carefully mapped by Fred Hartley. In fact, the mediaeval outline very nearly approximates to the outline of the present village. Modern mechanical ploughs with their steel blades, digging deeper than ever before, and pushing earth outwards in both directions, have obliterated many of the ridge and furrow fields

There are other transfers and buying and selling by individuals or groups of religious. Among the individuals noted are Samson de Leke (1247), Hugh de Despencer, killed at the Battle of Evesham in 1265, Ralph Palmer (1280), Thomas of Lincoln (1304), John Tack (1304), Alice of Ashby (1304), John of Seagrave who helped in the knighting of the king's eldest son, Edward of Woodstock (1346), and John of Ashby (1346).

On one Sunday in each year each parish had to make a collection for 'Peters Pence'. This money went to Rome, and went towards the running of the affairs of the Church. As a global organisation the costs were considerable. The Popes were regarded as monarchs, and the Cardinals as Princes of the Church, with all the rights and privileges accorded to them in other countries. In 1334 the Rectory paid two shillings in Peters Pence.

In 1452 Anthony Malory of the family of Malory of Walton was Lord of the Manor. He died in 1512, and Henry Malory, who followed him, died in 1533 leaving five daughters as co-heirs - Anne, Eleanor, Elizabeth, Margaret and Katherine. Lords of the Manors of South Croxton did not necessarily live in the village. For most of this period it was probably far too insignificant a place for that. We know that in 1563 there were only 32 families here, a population of about 144 - it is standard practice to multiply an adult population by 4.5 to get a rough guide to the number of people. A dwelling for a family at that time would have been on one floor, with two rooms, one known as the hall of the house, and the other as the parlour or chamber. It would have been timber framed and about the size of a small cottage.

W.G.Hoskins has written (see Ch. 3 'Quotations') that in about 1515 John Palmer of South Croxton was well above the average husbandman. His farmhouse had a buttery, as well as a hall, chambers and kitchen, and his personal estate came to £23.5s.6d. The livestock were worth considerably more than the crops (£9.6s.8d. as against £6.6s.8d); there were 80 sheep and 13 cattle. 36 acres of crops were sown, giving a total arable area of 54 acres including the fallow fields. Peas, always the most important crop in Leicestershire, covered 16 acres, and wheat and barley the remaining 20: again no rye or oats were grown. The total land, including pasture was about 90-100 acres. The number of the livestock would vary through the year, and we do not know at what time of the year the inventory was taken. Although the number noted might seem small, we must remember that when winter approached the beef cattle would be slaughtered and salted. The number kept depended on the amount of winter feed available. As a guide, the present level of livestock stocking in Leicestershire would be one cow or two sheep per acre.

In a record made between 1533 and 1538, W.G.Hoskins tells us with out further reference in a paper read to the Leicestershire Archaeological Society, no date, that there was a dispute which reached the High Court of Chancery in London. It involved two ordinary families, and was over just 4 acres of land. Edward Palley and his wife Joan were involved. At a time when hardly anyone but the clergy could read or write, records were kept in memory rather than on paper. Thus, Edward and Joan could recite the history of Joan's family going back through seven generations to the 14th.century. Joan, the court was told, was the daughter of John, son of William, son of John, son of Margaret, daughter of Agnes, daughter of Robert Randolf, husbandman, who had possession of the land. Hoskins found that John Randolf appeared in the Poll Tax returns of 1377, and 50 years earlier a John Randolfes paid two shillings towards the tax levied in 1327. The name 'Randolfes' became 'Randall' later, and for centuries they were shown as tenants of the manor.

As is noted in the chapter on the history of the Church, in a will dated 1686 Richard Woollaston left an amount of money 'for the relief of need' in the parishes of Barsby, Billesdon, Cold Newton, Loseby, South Croxton and Twyford. A note from 1835 says that, acting for the trustees, Col.Burnaby 'lays it out in flannels, sheeting, cloth stuffs and shirting as the necessities of respective Parishes require.' They are given to the 'most deserving poor'. However, 'to prevent the sale of coats and to distinguish the objects of charity, the cloth is dyed green and the letters 'W.C.' are engraved on the buttons. There is a note of a band proceeding to the Church, followed by persons wearing these coats. More recently, every pensioner in the villages received a donation on November 1st., and another year all the widows. There has been discussion among the trustees about whether these offended against the purposes of the trust, and what other means of identifying those in need might be found.

<u>*Enclosures*</u>

In the 18th century came the enclosures. By the 16th century most farmers rented a small amount of land from large landowners. They also owned a few animals which were allowed to graze on the common land of the village. Prior to the enclosures farming was organised in an open field system, crops being rotated between three fields, the Upper field, the Middle (east) field and the Nether (west) field.

There was a rapid growth in the cloth trade. This resulted in a great demand for wool. As prices grew it became more profitable for large landowners to switch from arable to sheep farming. Farmers began enclosing their fields with fences and hedges and filling them with sheep. Whereas growing crops involved employing large numbers of farm labourers, sheep farming needed very few workers. The gentry also required parkland for hunting, which entailed enclosing the bits of field.

In 1757 the 611 acres of Nether Manor was enclosed without an Act of Parliament, by agreement with the three owners, one of whom was a Pochin, but the Upper Manor waited till 1794 till an Act of Parliament compelled it to enclose its 111 acres. Commissioners were sent to every village and farm to establish the enclosure. W.G.Hoskins says that "When the parishes of Barsby and South Croxton were enclosed in 1798, the public roads were laid out mostly afresh". When new roads past the enclosed land had to be established, the commissioners laid their rulers on their map and drew them in. The Ridge Mere, the pre-historic path which came into the village to the west, stayed, and went through the village as before, and the road from Beeby joined up to it. The main road originally went up the hill as now, skirted the raised churchyard, which had existed before the road, went further up the hill around the field which held the moated site, and now the electricity sub-station, and then followed the present footpath through the stables, towards the Queniborough Road by the site of Court Close, and entered Barsby behind the former King William public house. This was the ancient path between the villages. In fact, the pathway continued on the other side of 'The Lane' as a green lane, hedged on both sides, and continued to the lost village of Newbold Folville and on to Gaddesby where it joins another footpath from Queniborough. The commissioners laid their rulers on their map and drew in new roads past the sub-station, straight down the hill towards the Queniborough Road, across it and up the hill to Barsby where it cut the Main Street in two at right angles. It continued down to meet the Ashby Road, itself also an enclosure road. The road from the Queniborough

Road down to the Hall and the lost village of Baggrave is also an enclosure road.

It is interesting to note that Nichols says that at the enclosures there were certain open fields within a common boundary in Barsby and South Croxton, which seems to give further weight to the notion that Barsby and the Upper lordship were regarded as a unit.

In 1775 there were 20 freeholders and 100 dwellings in the village. The Nether(South) Lordship was owned by Sir Charles Sedley.

In 1782 Thomas Hunt was born. The Internet tells us that he was an ancestor of the Angrave family. His son, Thomas (1806?-1840) was a loom hand, his daughter Mary (1834-1869) was a hose seamstress and died in childbirth, and the child, Mary (1869-1919), was brought up by her grandparents. There is also mention in the Thacker Towers Archive on the internet of Thomas Hunt, 'late of South Croxton', who in 1838 had stolen five elm boards to the value of three shillings from Thomas Ward. At the General Quarter sessions held at Leicester Castle he was fond guilty and sentenced to six weeks hard labour in the County House of Correction. It is not known whether this is the same Thomas Hunt mentioned above.

The predominant underlying material of the area is boulder clay, and the land was therefore used mainly for grazing. In the crop returns of 1801 we find that only one acre of peas were grown in the parish, which was by then growing in size. There were also 127 acres of wheat, 2 of rye, 60.5 of barley, 54 of oats, 3 of potatoes, 52 of beans and 26 of turnips in a total arable area of 326 acres. They show that less than half of the 700 acres available were used for arable farming, and when later directories were published the principal occupations of the inhabitants were farmers and graziers.

Cottage Industries

From before the beginning of the 19th.century cottage industries began. Evidence of this is in the record of the Hunts, as previously mentioned, and in the gazetteer published by Curtis in1831. At that time the parish contained 1,400 acres, and had 361 inhabitants, living in 63 houses, and expenditure on the poor rate was £158.7s. Some of the inhabitants were employed in framework knitting. This would doubtless be for the clothing manufacturers of Leicester. The framework-knitting period was of relatively short duration. It started at the beginning of the 19th.century. In 1844 there were 35 frames in the village, but had declined in the second half of the century. This relative affluence is reflected in the population of the period, where it hovered around 300, declining to 251 by 1891, and declining even more after that. At the present time, in comparison, there are 234 in the 2001 census return, with 43 under 18 and 9 under 4yrs. 70% of the adults work in service industries and many commute.

During the 19th. and into the 20th. centuries, South Croxton was a noted centre for the production of Stilton Cheese. Each farm had its own dairy room, and Freda Elliott's mother knew each of them, because she had worked in most of them. There are no dairy farmers left in the area, and cheese making stopped long ago.

Ordnance Survey map of 1896

The Ordnance Survey Map of 1896 shows a small settlement, made up of several clusters of development strung out along Main Street. There was obviously the Church and North Manor Farm shown at the top of the hill, a small cluster on each side of Main Street further down the hill, another group beyond Kings Lane, and a final cluster round Manor Farm. There was another cluster at the end of what is now School Lane. This pattern of development, flowing down the hillside, has given South Croxton a distinct linear form, broken in some places by the intrusion of open fields, such as north of Kings Lane and around the brook. The group of houses at the end of School Lane was, as has been mentioned, called 'Westhorpe' and was always separated from the main village by open ground, until the development of School Lane in the 70s.

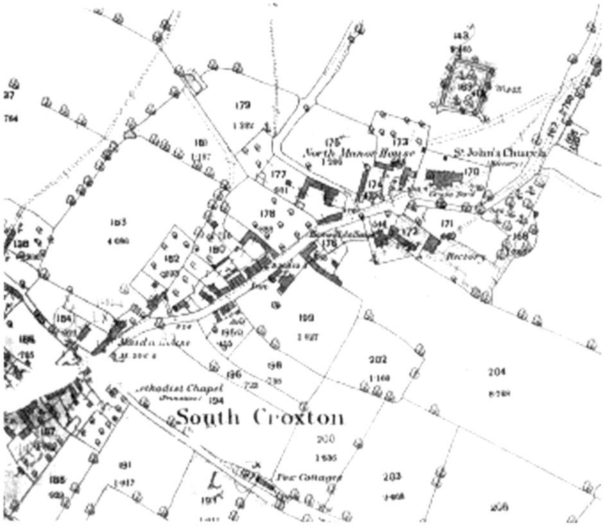

<u>*Further records*</u>

On May 10th 1980 a tin roof was removed from Bank Cottage in School Lane. Below it was the old thatched roof, largely intact, though the wooden base below was rotten. Bits of a newspaper were found which had been used to pack a hole when the thatch had been put on. It was the Daily Mercury of April 1878; they had offices in St.Martins, Leicester and had four editions a day. A news item notes that Samuel Walker of South Croxton was had up before the magistrates for an offence on his premises in the village. He had been selling, or selling unlawfully, at his licensed premise in the village. He had been celebrating a special event, he claimed, which had got out of hand. He was given a fine or 14 days imprisonment. Part of the report was missing, so we do not know which he chose.

In August 1898 a sale of work, opened by Mrs.Walker of Ratcliffe Hall, was held in a marquee next to the Rectory, raising £29.9s.0p. for an organ for the Church. The Deaneries' Magazine notes that 'many kind neighbours and good friends' had given money for this purpose, and countless contributors rose to the appeal of the unnamed organist. The October issue notes that the total to be spent, 'including the cost of the Organ', was £30.10s.4½. The deficit was £1.1s.4½p. which was paid off by Mr.Smith-Carrington of Ashby Grange. The organ would probably have been installed shortly afterwards.

Lance Corporal Weldon Shot in Ireland

In 'History of the 1st and 2nd Battalions of the Leicestershire Regiment in the Great War by Col.H.C.Wylly, C.B., pub. Gale & Folden, Aldershot', p.101, the author says:

'On June 22nd, 1921. His Majesty the King opened the Northern Ireland parliament in Belfast and appealed to all Irishmen to combine together in the endeavor to secure peace; while later the Prime Minister invited the heads of the Government of Northern Ireland and the leaders of Sinn Fein to meet and discuss matters at a joint conference in London. An agreement as a basis of discussion was drawn up, and on July 11th a truce was proclaimed between the Supreme Government and Dail Eireann, all operations against the rebels coming to an end on that date; the truce was, however, not religiously observed by Sinn Fein, for in the same month Lance-Corporal Weldon of the Battalion was murdered in the streets of Castlerea. The negotiations which now commenced were at once broken off.'

Lance-Corporal Weldon came from South Croxton, and was buried in Castlerae.

Electricity

Electricity came into the village in 1932, and Bob Parker put electric light and heating into the church in 1936. He also put electricity into The Grange for £16. Bob ran the garage, which stood near the top of the hill for a while.

Nathaniel Glover

A long article was published in the Leicester Mercury on Thursday January 20th. 1938 about old customs in the village. They were remembered and described by Nathaniel Glover, whose picture appears in the article - the top half of the picture below:

Nathaniel Glover 1858-1939

When Nat was born in 1858, it was the custom to put an egg the baby's hand, saying, "I wish you a houseful of meat". At the age of five he was thought ready to earn his living, so he would scare birds from the fields with a pair of clappers for four pence a day. Sometimes he would earn a few more pennies by opening gates for traps – a horse drawn open carriage. A carrier would take passengers into Leicester, and return twelve hours later, but young Nat, at five and six years, would walk the journey with his mother.

Those who went to school walked to Barsby, but Nat had no time for that. He later followed his father, who rose at 4a.m., worked 18 hours a day, with an extra shift on Sundays. Nat thought nothing as a boy of getting up at 5a.m., working 16 hours a day for 6 shillings a week, plough driving. Like other women of the village his mother would go into the fields cutting corn with her sickle, and gleaning so that her family would have enough flour. Perhaps five or six women would do this, taking a kettle to boil in the fields, returning in the evening, knocking the corn out of the ears, and take it to the miller to grind. Bread came from Rearsby in those days. The baker in this village baked puddings on Sundays and joints of meat for the villagers.

Food came to the table on pewter dishes in those days, until they were replaced by tin plates with the alphabet round the rim. There were framework knitters in the village, and two fetched their loads from Leicester, and returned them when completed. In the spring wild flowers filled Barkby Holt and the Prince of Wales' covert, and lined the sides of the brook between South Croxton and Baggrave. No one was allowed in the Holt or covert, but the young Nathaniel picked basketfuls of bluebells in Ashby Pastures.

Another delight was to go "cow-slipping" with his mother. They would return with a full load, and sit for hours picking the full flower out of the "snuft", setting aside the pips for the wine. It was profitable labour, 8oz.of pips to the gallon, at 1s.a gallon. With 15 or 20lb. of cowslip pips, Nathaniel would walk with his mother, and two or three old South Croxton women all the way to Humberstone Hall to sell their load to the Pagets. Once there, they would be bidden into the servants' hall, treated to a generous spread and a big jock of ale - "above two quarts, perhaps". That was in Queen Victoria's time, when women wore crinolines and poke bonnets, and all the village curtseyed to the gentry. They would return to the village, perhaps in time to hear the nightingale singing – "quite plainly at 9p.m. or 10 when you think all the birds are nesting." There might be gypsies camping in Holt Lane - lots of them - and

perhaps they would see the village witch walking about with no hat all by herself.
On May Day the children would sing round the maypole, and deliver baskets of flowers to every cottage.

Another welcome holiday was Whitsun, with its club feasts, and the Punch and Judy show, and the roundabouts (on the paddock behind the Golden Fleece).

November brought the "stattis", or fairs at Loughborough and Syston, "when servant girls and servant chaps were hired for 12 months", and danced together at the Golden Fleece. Melton Martinmas Tuesday was another chance for hiring.

Then came Christmas, when boys brought home the Yule log, coals were given to the poor of the parish, and a party of men went Christmas singing.

On the last day of the year hounds met opposite the manor as they do now (in 1938). Next came Plough Monday in January, when men dressed up, blackening their faces with soot from their own chimneys. Sometimes Leicester lads would come "ploughboying" - lads who didn't know what a plough was. Nathaniel's father dressed up as a woman, singing a song with the others, and old farmers would give them a drink and a tip.

Nathaniel grew up and became an all round man - a gardener and agricultural worker. He planted thousands of trees in Ashby Folville, and many different kinds of trees in the big spinney, knowing the ways of each like any expert.

A Parish Meeting elected him Constable, giving him a truncheon for his pocket and a pair of "bracelets" for offenders. "But I never had no cases." "That was disappointing," I asked. He laughed, not telling.

The apple tree in the wheelwright's yard played a part. The custom of "rantanning" offenders against the social code prevailed in South Croxton. Everybody knew about the misbehaviour, and an effigy was made of the culprit. A bag filled with straw, tied in the middle with an old hat on top, was hoisted into the tree and set alight. While this was going on the onlookers consumed 18 gallons of beer.

Nat Glover had more tales to tell. The most remarkable farmer in South Croxton in the 1890s was William Nuttall who worked the Manor Farm. It had 400 acres, and he always tried to milk 100 cows, but curiously one died every year, so his total was usually 99. He made Leicester cheese with the milk, taking it to Leicester Fair in May and October in the 1860s. He once took 14 tons of cheese - 7 wagon loads, and the detailed account of its loading and travelling and selling is vividly told by Nat. Tollgate keepers charged 4 pence a wheel after 11p.m. at the top of Checketts Road, and journeys were adventurous.

Nuttall had a seven acre field of cabbages, and employed 40 men to hoe it - 20 Englishmen and 20 Irishmen. (No man was ever sent away from Manor Farm who asked for work.) “Where do we go when we’ve hoed this?” asked one. “You go to the other side and start again,” was the order.

The wonderfully dry Summer of 1848 resulted in 18 days threshing. Labourers had only 2s.6d. a day (25p.) for carrying straw and corn, but were given as much ale as they could drink.

In 1871 came the remarkable flood with its amazing rescues. ‘And what must George Brien do but climb the notches of Queniborough Church spire and tie a silk handkerchief to the top. Don’t forget blind William Kirk. He foretold the weather for three months from March 21st. and December 21st. by asking where the cock on the spire was facing on those dates.’

Nathaniel Glover died, and was buried on February 14th.1940 aged 82 years. In a newsletter Rev.F.G.Clark wrote:
‘It is with much regret we record the passing of our old friend and servant, “Nat”, as we loved to speak of him. No more shall we see his slim figure slowly wending its way up the hill to the Church services or do the special “jobs” in the Churchyard that were his special care. Happily his end was not a painful one, but came very peacefully to him, although for many months past he was unable to take nourishing food. Of him, it can be truly said, as the

Rev.Wynn Watkins (Rector 1926-1934) said at his funeral service, "He was a good living man and a true friend." He was quiet and unassuming in all his ways, always friendly and ready to see the humour in life. His long residence in the village enabled him to supply me and other Rectors much information concerning the Church that was unobtainable elsewhere. His great pride was the Oak Door, and every year from the time it was made by his wife's father he made a pilgrimage to oil it. Truly, Croxton owes him much, and is the poorer for his passing."

Wartime

Before and during the war, Fred Draycott says, every cottage had a pig. Lesley Knapp at Hill Top Farm was the butcher. You took your pig up the hill with a rope tied to one leg. Lesley would get it on to a low table, and slaughter it. The blood would go to make black pudding, and 'everything would be used except the squeal'. In those days there was 'pigs fry' - liver, heart and lights fried up - and when you took round some swill to someone's cottage, you'd hope they would give you a helping of pigs fry.

While the village lost six men in the First World War, they lost none in the Second. Like much else, it almost passed the village by. There is a photograph of a platoon of Home Guard; down The Ridgemere there were Nissan huts containing shells; and an Anti-Aircraft battery. All the large houses around were taken over by the military. At Baggrave there were the Pioneer Corps; there was an American army camp at the top of the hill in Gaddesby, and another near the brook at Ashby Folville; at Lowesby there was the Red Cross. At the Hall in Gaddesby there were many meetings at a very high level. It was said of one married lady that she went out frequently in the evenings, '...but she never went out without her raincoat, whatever the weather'. Of course, who said it of whom I forget.

At this time both the Beeby Road and The Ridgemere were gated roads, with three at the village end of the Beeby Road, and four before New York Farm on the Ridgemere. Boys from the village would earn pennies opening them for the few cars that came through, and for the hunts that met regularly in the season.

Sale of Baggrave Property

In 1945 Baggrave was held by a retired Lieutenant Commander, H.E.Burnaby. In the early medieval period Baggrave was held by the Knights Templar of Rothley Termple. In 1543 it was granted by Letters Patent from the Crown to Frances Cave and his heir before it passed to Sir John Coke, Secretary of State to Charles I. John Edwin purchased it in1680, and rebuilt it, and it passed to his daughter Anna, who was married to Rev.Andrew Burnaby of Asfordby in 1770. Their eldest son, Edwyn Andrew, became a J.P. and Deputy Lord Lieutenant of Leicestershire. The Burnabys then owned the hall until about 1950. H.E.Burnaby decided to sell a number of properties in the village Among these was Ivy cottage in Main Street, at that time rented by H.L.Knapp at £18 a year. As a sitting tenant he purchased it for £485, plus various amounts for fees, searches and insurances. An Irishman, Bill Mitchell, had lodged there for a number of years. Subsequently, on the death of Margaret, Knapp's widow, she requested that he be allowed to remain living there. He worked for a flooring firm, and over the years the fumes from the glue it used affected his lungs so that he was forced to retire from ill health. His health deteriorated so that he had to have oxygen, and could not get up the stairs. His lounge was a maze of cylinders and pipes. Every Sunday he walked slowly up to the Golden Fleece at lunchtime. He had been such a good customer over the years that when a new sign was painted, he was given the old one. He died in 1994.

A blacksmith's forge had been located at the side of the Golden Fleece, and was approached through an archway in what is now the kitchen of the pub. In 1947 the smithy closed, the archway blocked, and the building was incorporated into the pub. A mounting block still stands at the former entrance to the smithy.

Water and Sewerage

In May of 1953 mains water came to the village. An article in the Leicester Mercury of Friday February 17th. 1953 said that an iron tank stood on tall stilts at the top of the village, it is still there, and that ten houses had been fitted with plumbing and shiny taps over sinks. The village had 21 wells, and a Ministry of Health official had found that 18 of them were polluted. This gave impetus to the villagers' claim that a clean water supply should be piped into the village. At the forefront of the campaign was the Rector, the Rev.Clarke, who sat on the Charnwood Borough Council. A sewerage system was introduced in 1966.

Water tank at the top of the hill

Advertiser article July 13th. 1957

A long article appeared in the Advertiser on July 13th 1957 in the series 'How our Villages got their names'. In it there is a photograph of Rev.F.C.Clark, the Rector, B.W.Payne, the postmaster, Bernard Kirk of Maida Farm, Mrs.Payne beside a cheese press, the Golden Fleece, School Lane towards the Golden Fleece, and the top of School Lane. It notes the field walk between Queniborough and South Croxton, along which crab apples could be picked, and mushrooms from a field. At the end of the walk 'a stately old lady', presumably at 'Barley Leys', served tea in her kitchen, and talked about Baggrave Hall as she knew it in her girlhood.' Her early memories were of Major Algy Burnaby at the Hall who ruled the Quorn hunt.

The Village Fete of 1964

On May 30th.1964 there was a Village Fete organised as part of the fund raising activities to replace the Village Hall, which at that time was a 1914 -18 Army Drill Hut, standing on the ground of the present 12 &14 School Lane. From the President's remarks printed in the programme it is clear that the original idea was to demolish the hut and rebuild a new village hall on that site. There was not enough room for parking on the old site, so the previous school was bought for that purpose. A programme of the event is located in the Village Archive, and more detail of the event in the chapter on the Village Hall.

.

The Village Fete, 30th May 1964, held to raise funds for the Village Hall

SOUTH CROXTON FETE

In aid of the Village Hall Building Fund

SATURDAY, 30TH MAY 1964

AT

ZION HOUSE

Commencing at 2.45 p.m.

To be opened by TED MOULT at 3-0 pm

PROGRAMME (admits to fete) 1/-

Keep this programme it may be lucky
in the draw for a basket of fruit.

The Pub and the Elliotts

On the corner of Kings Lane was a cottage occupied by Lucy Muggleton. There is an aerial photograph showing her garden. In the late 50s it was owned by Ruddles, the Rutland brewery, which also owned the Golden Fleece. When Lucy died, her cottage was incorporated into the pub, and is now part of the bar.

Freda and Jim Elliott behind the bar, circa 1960

In 1956 Freda and Jim Elliott took over as landlords of the Golden Fleece. What is now the restaurant was the bar, and what is now the bar was the restaurant. Freda did all the cooking, and Jim was famous as a hospitable and gregarious landlord, never short of a story, and excellent company. He had suffered from polio earlier in his life, and walked with a stick. The Golden Fleece grew in popularity; many annual dinners were held there, including that of the local Police, and it was famous for its 'lock ins', when, as 'time' was called, nobody could come in, but the doors were locked, and the partying went on till the early hours. At Christmas time turkeys could be bought there, and during the year rabbits and pigeons. The pub was also used as a bank, because many villagers would cash their cheques there. It is this era that is remembered most fondly by many who traveled from Leicester, and further, to drink there. Since the Elliotts left, there have been nine landlords, some lasting only a short while. During this period the pub has been transformed so that it could be in almost any locality in England. Its situation, décor and furniture are excellent, and it deserves to succeed. Having lost the school and the shop and Post Office, it would be a blow to the village to be without a pub, although there was a period of nine months when there was no buyer, and it remained shut.

As a footnote, the author was interested to meet John Leatherland, the great-great-great grandson of Joseph Leatherland (b1775). Thomas Leatherland's son Joseph ran the Golden Fleece in 1846. John visited the pub in June 2007, with his sister and their spouses. He was of the opinion that the mounting block outside, presumably used when the end of the pub was a smithy, was a concrete covered cheese press. This was used to cause the curds to mat together to make a single block of cheese.

Mounting block outside the Golden Fleece

There are two indentations front and back of the block where wooden uprights would have gone, and across the top of them would have been another piece of wood which held the corkscrew mechanism which drove a square piece of wood down to press the cheese. Certainly the sides look as if they are covered wooden slats. The mounting block, a physical link with the smithy, has now also become a link with the Stilton cheese making for which the village used to be famous.

<u>The Pottery</u>

In former cow sheds attached to Zion House Marion Aldis opened the Pottery in 1969, which was a thriving business concern. Later, she replaced the cowsheds by a purpose built pottery on the frontage of Zion House. It is now a 3 bedroomed residence.

<u>Further Records</u>

In March1969 a 200 year old link between South Croxton and the Kirk family broke. Mr. and Mrs.Bernard Kirk, last of that family in the village, left after farming 38 years at Maida House Farm. They went to Dorking in Surrey.

Alf Barsby, another old-timer had been born in no 83 Main St., the middle of the three cottages that now comprise Triple Cottage at no.85. When the three cottages had been converted into one and modernised in 1985, I took him round to show him. I took him into the main bathroom, and he shook his head and said, "Four of us used to sleep in a double bed in here." I then took him outside. He said, "It's a long time since I was in this back yard." I felt the spirit of Tony Hancock, never far from the surface, well up, and I thought to myself, "A back yard! This is a patio, mate." Alf lived in the village all his life, ending up at 64, Main Street, next door to Sid Coultate. Sid was to write an appreciation of Alf for this book, but sadly he died before he could complete it.

In June 1974 a mediaeval coin was found in the Rectory grounds. It was a silver half penny of long cross type, after 1279, possibly from a London mint - CIVITAS LONDON - though the inscription is difficult to read.

In September 1976 there was an article in the Advertiser about the rag dolls that Maude Nicol used to make to order. They began as dolls for her own children, Sheena and Linda, when they were small. Others saw them, asked her to make one for them, and the little business flourished. They were sold at the W.I.markets at both Syston and Melton Mowbray. Her daughter Sheena was at the time a nurse at the Royal Infirmary and working on the children's ward. A girl would not go to sleep without her doll. It turned out to be one of her mother's. Maude was also an accomplished painter, and had her paintings selected for exhibition at the South Croxton Arts Festival. One, a view of South Croxton, was selected for a County calendar. There is another cutting, perhaps from the Advertiser, but undated, noting the talk that Jim Nicol had given to the W.I. Jim was at the Technical College, the forerunner of the Polytechnic, itself eventually becoming the De Montfort University, at which he lectured in Maths. He had led a rescue expedition in Derbyshire two weeks previously, and related his experiences there down a pothole, where, sadly, a student had died. Jim was formerly an engineer from Aberdeen, but almost accidentally turned to lecturing. He was responsible for setting up the first computers in the then Technical College.

On several occasions Marion Aldis wrote and directed plays which were performed by the children of the villa and staged in the Village Hall. One such was 'Dr.Who' performed on 7th.June 1977 in celebration of the Queen's Silver Jubilee.

In 1989 Prince Charles came to the assistance of the wife of the Hunt Master, who was Mrs.Murray Smith, when she fell from her horse in the village, knocking herself unconscious

In the same year the Parish Council was established, replacing the Parish Committee. Sid Coultate, who had been Chair of the Parish Committee, was elected to do the same job on the Parish Council. Norman Hanford became its secretary, a post he held conscientiously until his unexpected death in 1993.

The Clarion, which had its first issue in 1989, carried a piece by Roger Moss in August 1998 which neatly summarises 'the saga of the lakes', a saga because it seemed to go on endlessly. To paraphrase: A field on the right at the end of the surfaced section of Kings Lane was purchased by a Mr.Fisk in about 1983. This had previously been part of the Baggrave Estate. It had a sloping, low lying section providing a natural drainage route from fields above to the brook below. The drainage was not a regular watercourse, but was rather a marshy depression bisecting the field.

Mr.Fisk added hardcore topping to the green lane extension of Kings Lane, and, using heavy earthmoving equipment, two lakes were formed, using the natural drainage water to fill and maintain levels.

Buildings were erected which, it was claimed were to be used for calf rearing and the housing of fish tanks to augment the fish breeding potential of the lakes. Mr.Fisk claimed that these were legitimate ‘agricultural’ enterprises, and thus permissible. Popular opinion was that the development was more likely intended to serve the commercial market for fishing and shooting, with the inevitable increase in traffic that would result.

Charnwood Council Planners decided that the development was clearly outside the scope of legitimate agricultural use and as no other application for other use and been received then the development was clearly illegal. A notice to reinstate the site to its original state was issued. Mr.Fisk filed for bankruptcy. He appeared before magistrates for not reinstating the site, and was fined £1,000. There was a considerable body of opinion in the village that the site should be reinstated, but that would cost a great deal of money. Mr.Fisk, a bankrupt, could not afford it. Charnwood Council could not afford it, with so many more deserving claimed needs to be met. Whichever bank is in receivership of the land would not afford it in order to sell. So there is an impasse, while the lakes become more absorbed into the surrounding countryside, becoming more overgrown and ‘natural’.

In 1990 a committee was formed to help John Redfern organise the South Croxton Arts Festival. It had not run that year because there were no catering facilities at the last moment. It continued with this support for another 12 years.

Reproduced by permission of Olwyn Hughes.

In her 'Sketchbook' column of August 2nd.1991, Olwyn Hughes sketched the village from Triple Cottage uphill. She remarked, "How fortunate we are to have such pleasing places as part of our national heritage."

Studies

In the Spring of 1998 Rachel Baxter presented 'A Geographical Study of South Croxton' as part of her GCSE Geography coursework. She identified reasons for settlements, their form or shape, and reasons for change. In the light of this she set out her aims for the study. She conducted her research by means of a questionnaire, transect mapping to determine land use, and as secondary research she consulted population figures, old photographs, and a geological survey map. A particularly useful map showed the dates on which individual dwellings were built. Another was a geological survey which shows deposits of sand and gravel beneath the topsoil north of the Church. A further interesting one showed the source springs and tributaries of the Queniborough Brook which originates near Tilton.

In 1999 Clare Stephens submitted a study of the changes in social structure of the village between 1851 and 1991 and the present day as part of her course work for her 'A' level Geography. She aimed to relate the movement into the village and employment, and looked at the age structure. Whereas in 1851 the villagers were employed locally in agriculture and manufacturing, in 1961 they had a wider skills base and related more to service industries. She looked at census reports, and conducted a survey of all the residents of the village. She found sound evidence to support, what had just been an hypothesis, that this was a dormitory village, though not a retirement one.

Further events

In 2000 the village received a grant from 'Better Villages Competition' launched by Leicestershire County Council and the Leicestershire Training and Enterprise Council. With this the brook was cleaned near the bridge, and two benches provided, at the top and bottom of the hill. The one at the bottom near the brook was designed and made by a villager, Bruce Attenborough.

In 2001 there was a proposal to buy the playing field behind the Village Hall. It was on a 21year lease at £183.00 per annum, subject to review. The Parish Council was offered it at £3,650. The PC sought a grant from Charnwood Borough Council to aid the purchase, the balance from the precept (the amount added to the Council Tax for the benefit of the Parish - lighting, etc.). The grant would be £1217.00, leaving £2,433.00 to find, an increase on the precept of £27.53 per household.

Also in 2001 all the members of the Parish Council resigned except one. The County Council administered it until a new council was elected under the chairmanship of Jeremy Delderfield. The post of Secretary was advertised, and Andrew Tatlow from Melton Mowbray was appointed.
The last Arts Festival was held in 2002. Poor weather resulted in

a much lower attendance than usual. Several people, including the Chair, had resigned from the Committee; John Redfern had withdrawn in 2000. There was nobody to be found to undertake the massive task of leading the committee and being at the forefront of organising the festival, so it ceased.

The following piece was in the Harper-Adams University web site in the summer of 2003:
'A straight 'A' student at Harper Adams University College, Shropshire, has been named the winner of the 2002 Dr Norman Gill Crop Science Award.

Mary-Kate Zillah Black, 22, from South Croxton, in Leicester, was named winner of the prestigious award, given annually to the best performing student on a crops management course, earlier this year.

Miss Black is currently a third year student on Harper Adams' BSc (Hons) Agriculture with Crop Management degree and has achieved an 'A' grade across the board in all modules and for both her written work and her employability whilst on her sandwich year industrial placement.

Miss Black attended a special awards ceremony held as part of Graduation Day in September to receive her award, kindly presented by Mr Ronald Jones.'

In 2003 in was noted by Fred Draycott that, when he did his annual tour of the village selling poppies at the end of October, just over 50 houses had been built within the village since the end of the war.

In September 2004 Sid Coultate died, and this should not go without mention. Sid had been a villager, with his wife Olive, since 1962 when he had his house built just down the hill from the remaining cottages. He was very active in the Village, being Chairman of the Village Meeting, and was referred to by the County Council whenever matters concerning the village came up.

As noted elsewhere (Road Names) he named 'Three Turns Lane'. When the Parish Council replaced the Village Meeting, he chaired that. He was also elected to serve in 2001, but had to resign because of ill health. Nevertheless, he attended all the annual Village Meetings. When his wife died he insisted on living on his own, although he was frail, and he could be seen each week making his way slowly and with a stick in Syston. Sid was a gentleman of the old school, invariably charming, humorous, gregarious and dapper. He will be sadly missed.

Jason Piper in Swan Lake

In November 2004 Brian and Annette Piper arranged for a coach load of villagers to go to the Birmingham Hippodrome to see their son, Jason, a villager, dance the lead, a menacing, seductive swan, in the Mathew Bourne all male version of Swan Lake. Jason became interested in dancing when the Leicestershire Schools Ballet Scheme visited his Primary school. He was also a rugby and football fan, a Tigers supporter, who left the Royal Ballet

School after two weeks because the tutors stopped him playing rugby. His teachers, Sue Rosenbloom and Val Egrie, said, "He knocks the idea of dance being effeminate on the head. What he does that's unique is to bridge the gap between male athleticism and the artistry of dance." His former Head at Judgemeadow, Anthony Green, said, "In rugby he could turn in the air. After Jason we had a set of boys who joined ballet classes." The performance was superb, and we were able to meet Jason afterwards and discuss the performance.

It was noted in the local press in June 2007 that Jason had been approached by the film makers of 'Harry Potter and the Order of the Phoenix', who had seen him in 'Swan Lake', about playing the role of Blane, a mysterious fortune telling centaur who despises humans. He will attend a cast screening this month before its release.

The website of the village was opened in May 2005 – www.south-croxton.org.uk. It was designed by Stuart Campbell, with text by Phil Snelders. Currently it contains pages on the village and its history, the history of the church, of the moated site, local groups - the WI and the Wednesday Club, Church news, containing a message from the Rector, and a list of services for the group of parishes, links to the local media, the bus timetable, other local village websites, Charnwood and Leicestershire County Council, the mobile library, local weather (very useful) and a map, and local medical services. It is hoped to develop the site in the light of comments from villagers and others. In September 2005 the site was refurbished, and a guest book added.

<u>*Queen Elizabeth Memorial*</u>

A village memorial was officially unveiled on Sunday June 5th 2005. Brian Piper has written about this elsewhere in this book. It is a monument designed to commemorate the Silver Jubilee of the Coronation of Queen Elizabeth II, and stands half way up the hill near a bench. It is in the shape of a pyramid covered with glazed tiles, each designed by a child. It is a unique monument in that it has been designed by the children of the village under the guidance of two local artists, Lisa Denham from Loughborough and Nita Rao from Mountsorrel. The delay had been caused, first because it was originally called a 'Village Sign', which to many called up images of East Anglia carved wooden signs at the entries to the village, such as at Barkby, second because there was misinformation about its size, and third there was much heated discussion about where exactly it was to be sited. At the top of the hill, by the brook, outside the village hall were all discussed and rejected. At last, though three years late, in a situation reminiscent of 'Clochmerle' by Gabriel Chevallier, it was finally unveiled half way up the hill in front of a large gathering of villagers.

The kindness and generosity of the village can be demonstrated by two recent events. In April 2003 the author had the opportunity to purchase from an air photography firm which was going into liquidation a set of aerial photographs of the village taken in 1981. He distributed a request for funds around the village, and before they had been completely delivered, a villager knocked on his door and handed him the full amount. Further sums came in, and although two additional photographs were bought, the total sum was exceeded by £52. There was one offer to purchase the photographs and to give them on permanent loan to the Village Archive, and two further offers to see what amount was collected, and any difference would be made up. The photographs were exhibited at the following meeting of the Parish Council. They are now available in the archive and on the Village CDRom.

The second occurrence was when there was a fire at the house of Peter Harris in Main Street. He was living there with his two teenage daughters, Rochelle and Charlotte, who were upstairs while he was cooking dinner on Christmas Eve 2003. In the lounge a log rolled off the fire and set the carpet alight. He heard the smoke alarm, opened the lounge door and was met by flames. He closed the door and went upstairs because he thought his daughters were still there. In fact they had come downstairs and had left the house. All were taken to hospital but were later released. They went to stay with his mother nearby, but soon were offered a cottage in the village while their house was repaired and redecorated. Meanwhile, however, their Christmas was ruined, as well as about £600 of presents destroyed. Philip Ciuffardi started a collection in the Golden Fleece, and he and his father, Gino, went round the village, and collected £608 to replace the presents. The event was reported on the front page of the Melton edition of the Leicester Mercury, and featured on the Nottingham broadcast of the BBC Midlands News

So this is South Croxton, a village that W.S.Hoskins loved to visit “at any time of the year”, a village that sometimes sinks into a quiet languor, then springs into life if need be. It remains one of the most pleasant and beautiful spots to walk through and to inhabit in the county.

Notes

1. The farm houses were, from the top of the hill: North Manor, Hill Top Farm, Gothic Farm, Woodbine Cottage, Maida House, 82, Main St., Ivy House, Zion House, South Manor, and The Grange.

2. W.G.Hoskins says this, but gives no reference or evidence.

3. Domesday - Leicestershire - 3, Lands of the Bishop of Lincoln; 13; 15, Lands of Robert of Tosny, 11.

View of the village reproduced by permission of Kate Jewell

2 Recent Research

More recent research by Vanessa McLoughlin, a Ph.D. student at the University of Leicester Centre for English Local History, has suggested that both Nicols (Antiquarian) and Pierce (Moated site) might have been mistaken in taking references to South Croxton to embrace the whole of the present village. From the earliest records there are references to the Upper End and the Nether (lower) End, that is, beyond the brook. Domesday has two accounts, possibly one for each side of the brook. During the enclosures the two parts were enclosed in different ways and at different times. There is a record of a piece of demesne (land for the Lord's own use) in Barsby, but not in the Upper end of South Croxton. However, John of Ashby held a Manorial Court in South Croxton in 1324, and by 1347 a charter reveals that there was a Manor House here, perhaps next to the church on the site of the present North Manor Farm. His son, John of Ashby, lived in the village early in the 14th.century. Many other 'Lords of the Manor' lived elsewhere. Of course, there are modern references to 'North Manor Farm' and '(South) Manor Farm'.

In ancient records, South Croxton is mentioned together with Barsby, and at other times with Barsby and Newbold Folville, a deserted village that lay in the fields to the west of Barsby. When it became deserted the fields were shared out between South Croxton and Barsby.

Different documents in the fourteenth century make sense if the land of Upper South Croxton were added to that of Barsby. Indeed, in the thirteenth century it seems as if the tenants of Barsby were overcrowded, and South Croxton had land to spare, and there was some sort of sorting out. In the early fourteenth century Barsby and South Croxton were regarded as a unit.

Ancient management of the open field system was very complicated. Courts were held to settle differences, and to organise communal farming activities such as scouring (cleaning) of a lane. Tenants of the court of the Soke of Rothley was one such court. Twice a year tenants of the two villages attended the Great Court of Rothley until the Dissolution. There were also small courts which could be held in any village in the Soke. These were less formal, and could be held in any suitable public open space, such as a village green. There is evidence that such courts were held in the townships of Barsby and South Croxton. But where? The open field system seems to have been managed as a unit between South Croxton and Barsby. If so, the day to day agricultural work would have to be organised, disputes about ownership settled, bequests acknowledged, rights and responsibilities laid down, and so on. The question is, where did this happen?

Nicols quotes the Rector, Philip Hackett, who recalled the land he rented in the parish, and it included an ancient close called Court Close on which stood a house '...where some court was held formerly'. Mr.Hackett then tried to find out more, but could not. This close is about half way between South Croxton and Barsby, and along its southern edge would have been the ancient way between the villages. The close is partly surrounded by banks and ditches. It has perhaps a platform area from which a crowd might be addressed. It would be fascinating to have a geophysical investigation undertaken to see if there were any archaeological remains there.

It is also significant that on a map of the ridge and furrow system made by Fred Hartley, Court Close and the three or four fields behind it, which would include the stopping off place for the drovers with their sheep or cattle, there is no sign of ridge and furrow disturbance. This suggests that in the time of the open field system, these fields were not tilled as the others were, but kept apart for their special purposes. There is another patch clear of ridge and furrow to the west of Barsby, and this would be where the abandoned village of Newbold Folville lay.

So, rather than suppose that the village was an entity, it might have always been split into two, with the upper part conducting its affairs in conjunction with Barsby, holding regular meetings, perhaps every three weeks, in a Close half way between the villages to allocate tasks to be done, organise the workers and the implements, and to settle disputes and keep order. Then, every so often representatives would attend the Rothley court, perhaps to give an account of what had been done and decided.

In the vicinity of Court Close are at least two other fields, which the Enclosure Award describes as 'ancient enclosures'. One is also a Close, the other is a Green. It is interesting to note that there was a drover's way, which approached the present road to Barsby; it is the present exit almost opposite the electricity sub station. By the electricity sub station is a pathway, which was its continuation, and which might have been wider in past years. It might have been that drovers would come with their cattle and sheep, and rest at the Green and other fields before continuing. As a stopping place for drovers, and a meeting place for the two villages, the area would have been a significant one.

Based on a conversation, a tour with, and a paper by Vanessa McLoughlin, discussions with Richard Fox of the Leicestershire County Council Archaeology Team, and some additional material.

85, Main Street, Triple Cottage

3 Some quotations about South Croxton

Some evidence of pre-historic occupation - "A curiously shaped flake, used as a scraper, discoloured as though by use, was found upon a gravel drive at South Croxton by the author.."
A.R.Horwood, in
Alice Dryden (ed.) Memories of Old Leicestershire p.59
1911 George Allen
(Of course, the scraper, presumably Stone Age, might have been imported with the gravel. (P.S.))

"From the Tilton uplands long finger like ridges reach out towards the Soar and Wreake valleys, and two of the most prominent of these are followed by roads of great antiquity. One, called Ridgemeer Lane, in its last stages runs by a footpath today just north of Cold Newton, and then along the top of the ridge by path and bridle roads past New York Farm to the edge of the Wreake flood plain near Syston. Parish boundaries follow this route for some miles, indicating that it already existed when the first boundaries were being drawn in pre-Conquest times.

Parallel to it along the top of the next ridge to the north runs another old way, passing above Lowesby and South Croxton and coming down to the edge of the plain at Queniborough. Both South Croxton and Queniborough have produced evidence of Bronze Age occupation, but the age of these two roads cannot be given with certainty beyond saying that they are pre-Roman."
W.G.Hoskins The Heritage of Leicester p.22
1972 City of Leicester Publicity Dept.

(Note: unfortunately Hoskins does not give any reference to the evidence for his last sentence, so at the moment we only have his word for it (P.S.))

The meaning of 'ridgeway' is an ancient upland route of pre-historic, i.e. well before the Roman invasion(43AD). 'Mere' is a

boundary (as Hoskins notes above)..
David Hey (ed.) The Oxford Companion to Local and Family History
1996 Oxford University Press

On the layout of new roads at the enclosures of the 1700s:

"When the parishes of Barsby and South Croxton were enclosed in 1798, the public roads were laid out mostly afresh."
W.G.Hoskins The Making of the English Landscape p.97
1957 Hodder & Stoughton
(Note: Queniborough Road and the Baggrave Turn are other examples of enclosure roads P.S.)

In the Records Offices there may exist - but in much smaller numbers - even more interesting maps which show the layout of the villages and its open fields, with every strip separately shown, and all the other features of the fields, as they were on the eve of the enclosure. It is a completely medieval picture. Superimposed on this map of things as they were, one sometimes finds the lines drawn in by the commissioners showing where they propose to create the new fields and hedges, and the new roads, public and private. One sees on such maps the new landscape actually in course of being planned, and one can see how completely it was drawn afresh, regardless of almost everything that had gone before. Such maps are rare. The Leicestershire Record Office possesses only two, from the parishes of Stathern (1792), and South Croxton and Barsby (1798). The Lincoln Record Office does not posses a single map of this kind, in an otherwise rich and varied collection of records. (pp.186-7)

It is sometimes said that the public roads laid out by the enclosure commissioners followed the lines of the mediaeval footpaths and bridle paths between the villages, paths that had been trodden out first in Anglo-Saxon times. But this is by no means always true. The strip map of Barsby and South Croxton, already referred to, shows the public roads of these two parishes to be laid out on almost entirely new lines. Here and there they pick up and make use of the old common balks in the former open fields, which must have been the usual way of proceeding form one village to another in open field country, but for the most part they are drawn straight across the old furlongs and strips regardless of all considerations but that of directness. (p.203)

Hoskins, W.G. The Making of the English Landscape
1955 (1st.ed.) Hodder & Stoughton, London

"Well above the average husbandman are John Palmer of South Croxton, and Robert Branwell of Drayton (no date, but probably 1510-20). John Palmer's farmhouse had a buttery, as well as a hall, chambers and kitchen, and his personal estate came to £23.5s.6d. Here again, the livestock were worth considerably more than the crops (£9.6s.8d. as against £6.6s.8d); there were 80 sheep and 13 cattle. Of crops there were 36 acres sown, giving a total arable area of 54 acres including the fallow. Peas, always the most important crop in Leicestershire, covered 16 acres of the 36 sown, and wheat and barley (not specified separately) the remaining 20: again no rye." (Noted in 1515).
W.G.Hoskins "The Leicestershire Farmer in the l6th.century - the Husbandman"
In Essays in Leicestershire History
1950 Liverpool University Press

In 1785, "Tilton was one of the localities with a reputation for witchcraft, along with the neighbouring villages of Twyford and South Croxton....The story goes that all the Twyford and South Croxton witches were destroyed when villagers saw them at dawn one morning. They were in the guise of cats and floating on the brook in a wooden bowl. The locals threw large stones at them, breaking the bowl and drowning the witches."
David Bell, 'Leicestershire Ghosts and Legends',
1992 Countryside books

The lordship is partly old inclosure, and part open field. The village stands about seven miles from Leicester and consists of 100 dwellings. The church has a nave, a side aisle, and a spire, steeple with four bells. In the chancel there is a stone to remember Elisabeth Pick, who died in 1773, and in the body of the church one to remember Mary Barnes, daughter of Richard Chamber, cfg: date 1575
John Throsby, Select Views in Leicestershire Vol.11 1790

Only South Croxton has produced evidence (Pearce and Mellor 1986) from well conducted excavations of settlements of the period (Anglo-Saxon). They were around a moat lying north of the Church and one of the Manor Houses, and revealed occupation of the 9th/10th centuries. The earliest structures were a clay and timber building, interpreted as a barn or store, and associated ditches and gullies. It seems likely that these were subsidiary to the proto-manorial site on the site of the later North Manor House. Although South Croxton does not look at first sight to be planned, the enclosure map of 1794 may suggest otherwise. A rectorial manorial 'module' can be discerned at the north end, including the Church, and an equally rectangular module can be seen below. The 8th/10th century ditches and gullies are on this alignment so if this is a planned settlement it is likely to be of this period. Planning is, however, difficult to prove - rectangular settlements may merely have fitted into the rectangular furlongs of a pre-existing field system.
Archaeology of Anglo-Saxon Leicester by Peter Liddle, in
Anglo-Saxon Landscapes in the East Midlands
Proceedings of the Conference held at the Leicester Museums and Art Gallery, Leicester, March 1991
Ed.Jill Bourne
Pub. Leicester Museums and Art Records Service

4 South Croxton Population

Domesday (including Quenby)
Sokemen (free peasant tenants in the Danelaw) 0, villeins (an unfree tenant of the Manor) 11, Bordars (a smallholder who farmed assorted reclaimed from woodland or waste land on the edge of the village) 6, servi (slaves, or an unfree peasant) 5, Franci genae (French born) 1 . Multiply by 4.5 to include families = 104

1377 Poll Tax 67 = 301

1563 Diocesan Return 32 households = 144

1603 Deanery of Goscote 130 communicants

1670 Hearth Tax - paying households 48, exempt 12 = 270

1676 Dearnery of Goscote 139 communicants

Census Returns

1801 185
1811 253
1821 316
1831 315
1841 297
1851 324
1861 311
1971 296
1881 251
1891 234*
1901 222
1911 211
1921 200
1931 221

1951 153
1961 188
1971 195
1981 213
1991 226
2001 234 and 43 of school age and 9 under 4yrs.

In 1884 Barsby Lodge (population 6 in 1891) was transferred to South Croxton, and part of South Croxton (population nil) was transferred to Barsby.

5 The Historic Road Names of South Croxton

The open fields of the Upper Manor of South Croxton (north of the brook) were enclosed by Act of Parliament in 1794 and the land allocated to various owners. As part of the Act, Public Carriage Roads, Private Carriage Roads and footpaths were also defined when they crossed the old open fields.

There were six defined “Public Carriage Roads” all to the North of the village. The main reference point was the crossroads towards Barsby which was known as “THE MOORDALE TUNNEL”: a corruption of this remains in the house name “Mowdales”. Of interest, although outside the parish, the road from the “tunnel” into Barsby was “BUSS SICK LANE” with “sick” meaning “meadow.

The roads east and west from the “tunnel” were just known as Twyford and Queniborough Roads. The other main names were defined by the name of the fields within the area contained by what we now know as Main St., Queniborough Rd., Three Turns Lane and the green lane beside the livery stables. These fields were known as the “Thurns” which is an old English term for a large field with many corners.

The road from the “tunnel” into the village (i.e. the north end of Main St.) was known as “THURNSIDE ROAD” and the green lane as “THURN LANE”. The road on the other side of “The Thurns” from the Queniborough Rd. into the village (now Three Turns Lane) crossed the westernmost Thurn called “Thurn Green” and therefore was called “THURN GREEN ROAD” for most of its length. From the turn by the end of the green lane (i.e. by the livery stables), the road became known as “PEAR TREE LANE” into the village.

As the Act only defined those roads across the open fields the streets within the village did not have to be specifically defined or named but there is reference to two private carriage roads which were created to allow access for landowners to the east and west of the village. The eastern one of these was known as 'NETHER END ROAD" and it began a short distance along what we now call King's Lane but which was then known as "NETHER END LANE".

Julian Duxbury

Note: Kings Lane was not named after a King, but after a large field half way down on the right, Kings Close. When the Methodist Chapel was erected in 1867 it was changed to 'Chapel Lane', and it reverted to its original name when the Chapel was demolished in 1951.

'Three Turns Lane' was so named by Sid Coultate, then the chairman of the Parish Committee, to distinguish it from 'Four Turns', or the crossroads on the Queniborough Road. The County had money to put up signs on roads which had none, and Sid was pushed to name it.

6 Shops

The village would have been self sufficient for many hundreds of years. Carriers from both Leicester and Melton Mowbray would have brought provisions into the village, and there would have been a means of distribution of food, leather, cloth, as well as of locally produced meat, dairy produce, bread, etc. Travelling peddlers would also have visited the village.

The first written record of any shop was in White's Directory for 1846. There were four shops in the village, probably in peoples' front rooms. Thomas Leatherland, who ran the Golden Fleece, was also a smith, and his smithy was where the kitchen in the present building is, and which was approached through an archway. The mounting block is still by the steps. He was also a 'victualler', a purveyor of food and other goods. William Wittrick was a grocer, Joseph Tunnicliffe a tailor and draper, and Edward Cooper was the baker, as well as being a shopkeeper, but there is no record of the kinds of goods he sold. His premises were at 89, Main Street. The present kitchen of the restored house would have extended well into the area now occupied by the garage of number 85, and would have been the bakery and shop. It would have been the place where the people in the village would have brought their Sunday joints to cook in the oven. It is curious that no boot maker was noted in this source.

Successive directories give names of shopkeepers, and of trades that might well have entailed a retail outlet of some sort - 'shopkeeper', tailors and a draper, carpenters, a wheelwright, shoemakers, grocers' carriers, dress maker, bricklayer, postmaster/mistress, maltster, and the bailiff to Baggrave Hall who lived in Fox Cottages.

We get information about the Royal Mail and the postmasters from 'The Royal Mail in Leics. And Rutland' by John Soer (1998):
'A daily post service from Thurmaston to Lowesby via South

Croxton started in 1847. At the same time a sub-office opened in the village with Thomas Line as 'Receiver'. His salary was £6 a year and included his delivery duties.
In 1864 the mail arrived in the village daily at about 11.15 a.m. via Thurmaston.
By 1867 the sub-office was vacant and a wall-box was substituted.
In 1876 the mail arrived at 9.30 a.m. via Houghton-on-the-Hill.
In 1894 the sub-office reopened with Tom Adams as postmaster followed by Mary Adams in 1896, Lionel Palmer in 1898 and John Smith in 1899.*
In 1905 the mail began arriving from Gaddesby by 'cyclepost'.
From 1912-25 the postmaster was Charles Smith.'

A piece in the 'Mr.Leicester column in the Leicester Mercury , January 13th.1996 shows a postcard of J.Langton's hat and cap warehouse sent to Mr.Smith, postmaster of South Croxton. A message on the back asked him to deliver half a cheese the next time he went into Leicester. The piece also continues; 'In addition to running the Post Office, Mr.Smith was involved in cheese making, and later developed the business when he moved to South Manor Farm.' This information came from Mr.Smith's daughter-in-law.

Man and dog walking past the Post Office on the left, about 1920.

Within living memory there was a shop and post office in the village, at 'The Homestead', 49 Main Street. Bernard Wheeler and his wife Kathleen came to the village in 1957 with their daughters, Margaret and Rachel. They bought 'The Homestead' from Jack and Sybil Barsby, brother of Alf Barsby, who had been born in 85, Main Street, and subsequently moved to 64, Main Street. At that time Bert Payne ran the post office from a cottage opposite the shop at 49, Main St., The cottage holding the Post Office was reported in the Advertiser of July 13th.1957 as one of the oldest in the village, a cruck building, with apparently the upper section of the crucks sawn off when the roof was raised. Mr.Pickup at the Malt Shovel Cottage ran a small shop selling mainly sweets. Kathleen Wheeler opened and ran the shop at 49, Main St. until her death in 1966, when Bernard Wheeler ran it in her place.

Village shop 1980s

He had been a printer in Leicester, but during his time in South Croxton had been self-employed, running a small holding on 'The Homestead'. In an article in the Advertiser of about 1984 he says that if it were not for the Post Office side of the shop he would close. 'I look on the shop as a service to the people of the village - it is my contribution,' he said.

The shop finally closed on the 31st.March 1988, and Bernard

moved to a bungalow at 16, Syston Road, previously occupied by Stanley Crawford, and lived there until his death on June 5th.1997 The Post Office element continued in the Golden Fleece, and in various houses, and opened on two mornings a week. It closed at Gothic Farm in 2003.

With the help of material from Julian Duxbury, and Margaret Gardner, daughter of Bernard Wheeler.

7 The Alehouses of South Croxton

Over the last 250 years South Croxton has had at least five alehouses or pubs in different locations around the village. The earliest records are for 1753 when there were three establishments operating. The first remained open for only another ten years and there is no firm indication of its name or location. However the name of the landlord was William Towers and some years later he was resident in one of the cottages on the site now occupied by 34, School Lane which could therefore be a possible site.

On the other two alehouses of the time there is much better information. The first was known as “The Mason’s arms” and was located in the Westthorpe area of the village - i.e. in School Lane. The precise location is yet to be determined but it is hoped further research may reveal it. “The Mason’s Arms” did twice close for a period of a few years but on both occasions reopened until its final closure in the 1850’s.

The third alehouse operating in 1753 was “The Golden Fleece” which remained open continuously. Its stability was perhaps due to it being a freehold with a series of long established landlords. The landlord in 1753 was William Brown who remained in place for another 35 years. The license then moved to William Goadby and then via his widow to her second husband Thomas Leeson for the next half century. Ownership then passed to the Leatherland family who held the pub to the 1890’s. It was then with a sale to the Leicester Brewing and Malting Co. that the pub became brewery-owned until its purchase in the 1950’s by the Elliotts from its then owner, Ruddle’s. The present façade dates from 1837.

In the nineteenth century two further alehouses opened. In the 1830’s came the Queen Adelaide which was located in close proximity to the Golden Fleece, perhaps at no.81/3, but the exact spot is not yet discovered. The landlord was Thomas Simpson who was also a grazier and landowner. The Queen Adelaide, like the Mason's Arms, closed in the 1850's.

The Malt Shovel.

In the same decade the last challenge to the Golden Fleece arrived in the Malt Shovel Inn.

The Malt Shovel (at 39, Main St.) did its own brewing on the site from 1823. The"brewster" was Thomas Brandard who moved in on that date. When the old brew house was knocked down during renovations in the 1960s, a brick dated 1824 was found. Perhaps it supplied other pubs in the village, but when two closed down in the 1850s, it opened as a pub. The source of the beer for the other alehouses is unknown but it is possible the Mason's Arms was supplied by a "brewster" who lived in Westhorpe. The Malt Shovel premises had had absentee ownership since 1817 and there were a succession of landlords through its life. Finally in May 1893 on the death of the owner the property was bought by the Leicester Brewing and Malting Co. for £500. In the following September the brewery sold the site on to Thomas Fairbrother of Twyford for £250 on condition that the premises never again be used for the sale of alcohol. Thus the monopoly of the Golden Fleece was secured.

Julian Duxbury

The Golden Fleece.

Note: In the early '80s, Ken Middleton, an artist and poet, wrote and published a poem called 'Mais ou sont les neiges d'antan?' (Where are the snows of yesteryear?) - a quotation from the work of a 15th.century French poet. The poem was about writing that quotation on the wall of a 'men's loo'. He writes, 'The 'men's loo' referred to belonged to the Golden Fleece pub at South Croxton, Leicestershire, as it was in the '70s. The graffiti had, at the time, acquired an almost legendary status.' Ken's poem is in the village archive.

The Golden Fleece

8 Archaeology

Round About

Hoskins says that Bronze Age remains were found along the Ridgemere and at South Croxton, but gives no further referencing.

Some Anglo-Saxon finds have been made near Baggrave - portions of buckets, hoops and staves dating from the 9th/10th centuries.

'Broad Stone'

Moody Bush Stone with 'MOO-' carved on this face, July 2005

'In a field off The Ridgemere is a stone of great antiquity. In Domesday times Syston was in the Goscote Wapentake, or Hundred. The County had four Hundreds, but two new ones were formed in 1346. One of them was the East Goscote Hundred, and Syston was in it.

The Court of this Hundred was held in Syston, and the village was important as a meeting place for all the villages in the Hundred. The court was held on Scandinavian lines, that is, under a tree or on a hill away from the village or town. The site at Syston was Mowde Bush Hill, Ridgemere Lane. This lane dates back to pre-Roman times, then being a rough track.

In the field on Mowde Bush Hill is a stone which stands four feet high, is five sided, and is inscribed 'MOO-DY-BUSH'. By this stone were the ancient East Goscote courts held.

Later the Court was transferred to Rothley (Mountsorrell). This transfer of power was signified by the Mediaeval Act of Enfeoffment (Enfeossment).

It is recorded in 1790 that, twice a year, the court was called at this large stone in Syston, and adjourned to Mountsorrell. The same day the court was held (it was arranged by Sir John Danvers) his Lawyer and Steward went to the Syston Hill and, after a ceremony, dug up a piece of turf, sprinkled it with water from the Holy Well of St.John in Syston, and then took it back to the court in Mountsorrell.' (Melton Mowbray Times, May 22nd.1952, author unknown.)

This act signified the reverence with which the original site was held. Representatives from South Croxton, being in the Soke of Rothley, would have attended the meetings at Syston to give an account of their decisions at Court Close (see chapter 'Recent Research'), and later at Rothley. When the author visited and photographed the stone in July 2005, the only inscription on the stone was 'MOODY', from the Saxon word 'moot', or assembly, from which we get our phrase 'a moot point' - a point up for discussion.

Interestingly, 'Syston' comes from the Old English 'sida stan', meaning 'broad stone'.

The Moated Site

Moated site and Church circa 1972

"Excavation of this moated area revealed a scatter of roofing slate and fragments of creased ridge tile, but no other evidence of structures. Excavation was carried out on two sides revealing a shallow moat, and earthworks to the south produced fourteenth century pottery. Beneath the earthworks two cobbled roads were found, one running to the southwest corner of the moat in a westerly direction and the other running north-south . Both were edged with glacial boulders and in filled with small cobbles. Thirteenth century pottery was found in one of the roads, and cart ruts on the north south road. Beneath this road and the surrounding area, eight large post pits, some drainage gullies and a large ditch running north south were found. All contained Saxo-Norman pottery (Stamford ware). Also found were four spinning whorls, a coin of Aethelred II, a gilt strap and a number of bones."
The work was carried out by T.Pearce for the Department of the Environment and Leicester Museums.
Transactions of the Leicestershire Archaeological and Historical Society Vol XLVII 1971-2; re-published in Archaeology in Leicestershire and Rutland ed. Alan McWhirr

This rather dry account hides a rather interesting story.

There is documentary evidence that in the later 13th.century Robert de Ashby was the principal landowner at nearby Quenby, and by 1304 had land, not only in South Croxton, but also in neighbouring Ashby, Barsby and Baggrave. His son John came of age not long afterwards, and tried to sell the estate in South Croxton. For some reason he was unsuccessful. But he held a Manorial Court in South Croxton in 1324, and by 1347 a charter reveals that there was a Manor House here. So having failed to sell the land, it seems that he decided to develop it, and this fits with the archaeological evidence, and fits the date of the rebuilt church, some time early in the 14th.century. John's grandson, John the younger, retired from Quenby to live at South Croxton in about 1330.

The estate remained in the hands of the family until the 18th.century, when because there was no male heir, it was split up, and the estate archive disappeared.

Before Robert's time, in about 1200, there was a large aisled building beyond the church and the Manor House. The roof was supported by wooden pillars sunk in potholes in the ground. There was no evidence that this building had been used as a grain store, but evidence of a hearth was found as well as evidence of general domestic activity.

In about 1250 this building was deliberately demolished; the posts were removed, the pot holes filled in and the site leveled in preparation for the next building. Channels were dug which would have held upright posts enclosed in clay tempered with chopped straw to protect the posts from rot. This building was erected straight after the previous building was demolished.

It was at this stage that Robert decided to carry out improvements. In its turn this building was demolished, and the purpose of the site completely changed. Two roadways at right angles, but not connected, were constructed obliterating the previous potholes and gullies. They seemed to be important roads, judging by their solid construction and careful edging. They were certainly constructed early in the 14th.century, perhaps contemporaneously with the building of the present church. Both roadways were constructed of crushed rock and stone mixed with compacted small stones and pebbles, and edged with rounded boulders. The north-south road was about 3 metres wide, and led off into the fields beyond the church. To the west of the road there seems to have been a standing area; the edging went along the road and around it. There would have been stores or barns nearby. Heavy loads must have come along it because deep ruts were found about 1.2 meters apart, which had cut through the metalled road into the earth beneath.

The east-west road was rather narrower, about 2.5 metres, and there is a 12.5 metre gap between it and the north - south road, marked with larger stones. They seem not to have joined up because there is no break in the edging of the north-south road. There is a suggestion that it might have turned south at this point. There might have been a building which separated them, but there is no evidence of this. Later in the 14th.century a further reorganization seems to have taken place, because this road seems to have been abandoned, and an unsurfaced track cutting across the west end of the disused road-way and heading for a point where the north-south road crossed a ditch. This track had a gully on its south west side.

The size and solid construction of the roads suggest the size and importance of the community at this time, and the resources available to it. This, with the reconstruction of the church and the presence of a Manor House, indicates the existence of a thriving community in the 13th.century.

The moat was dug in the 15th.century, after the main period of moat construction in the country. The trees which are to be seen today were planted after 1794. An enormous amount of time and effort must have gone into its construction. The spoil from it was used on the moat platform, and to level out much of the surrounding area, including the excavated site to the west. Why such an expenditure of time and labour was made is unclear. It did not surround and protect the Manor House - there was no evidence of a building found within the moat, and it is assumed that the Manor House stood on the site of the present North Manor farm. It is too far from the Manor House to be a moated garden or orchard. It is possible that because there was internal unrest in the area, villages were likely to be at the mercy of marauding bands of soldiers. The moated site might have been a place in which to store grain and stock until the danger had passed. The enclosed area would have perhaps been too small for this purpose. The moat would also have been an excellent source of fish; and it has been suggested that this was its sole purpose.

Very little new evidence was uncovered by the archaeological excavation, but it all fits in with, and corroborates the documentary evidence. This is the only evidence in the County of Anglo-Saxon settlement based on well-conducted excavations.

It is interesting that in the Advertiser report of July 13th.1957, it is recorded that the grandfather of Bernard Kirk, who would have been born early in the 19th.century at North Manor Farm, could remember it having a moat and a drawbridge, though he might perhaps have been confusing North Manor with the Moat

The Moated Site is a Scheduled Ancient Monument.

Further excavations

While in the village, Terry Pearce unofficially investigated two other areas, he told the author. There had long been a tale in the village that in the field behind what is now called 'The Old School House' there had been a battle in the Civil War, and that some of the dead were buried by the solitary tree that grew in the middle. He carried out some investigation, but did not officially record it. It was evident that there had been a previous excavation at some time, and a dismembered skeleton, perhaps of a cow, and a sheet metal undefined object were uncovered. Was this the source of the tale? No bodies were found, only evidence of osier beds - osier is a kind of willow used for basket weaving.

He also investigated some curious configurations near the brook, and found that they were ancient watercress beds. The river must have been flowing fairly strongly, not only to flow through the watercress beds, but also to turn the mill that Domesday tells us was thereabouts (of course, it might have been somewhere else, and not on the Queniborough Brook). It would not have been a windmill because these were not introduced until the 12th.century. The site of such a mill has not yet been found.

'Roman Road'

It has entered local folklore that bits of a Roman Road keep being dug up by Frank Black in his fields to the north of the village. He has never claimed that these were Roman. If they were, the problem arises where it came from and where it went. The likelihood is that it is a metalled road through the fields to assist in the transfer of crops to storage sheds or barns. These roads would be similar to those found in the excavation of the moat.

The moated site from Church tower

9 The Church of St.John the Baptist, South Croxton

Taken July 2004. Note the 12th century roofline clearly visible on the tower.

The present church

The present church stands nearly at the top of the hill with only the moated site beyond it. It dates mostly from the 14th.century. It was built in the first half of that century, was built in the style of the age, with thinner walls than the previous church, with larger windows, and a more decorative exterior. The Norman church, on the site of which it was built, was not completely abandoned, for there is evidence of some Norman foundations. At the refurbishing of the structure in 1925, remains of Norman foundations for a North aisle were discovered, so perhaps the foundations of some of the church are Norman. The Norman font was placed in the new church, given a 14th. century octagonal base, and is still in use.

The Norman font.

The church seems to have been built in a pre-fabricated way; pieces were probably brought in from other demolished or rebuilt churches. Some of them might have been from the Norman Church built in 1087, like the font and rounded chancel door, or a Saxon one before that, like the stone slabs in the porch or the Saxon carving in the south aisle. The windows on neither the north nor south side are a set; the arch below the tower was constructed for a much larger tower and spire than now stands there. On the north wall by the tower arch there is the beginnings of an arch, possibly for a north aisle which was abandoned. In the north wall of the chancel there is a rounded Norman door, out of keeping with the Early Decorated style of the rest of the building. It all adds to its character.

The church comprises a West tower with a short spire, a nave and south aisle and a chancel. It is built of crumbling ironstone, with many mollusc fossils buried in it, and with square hewn freestone (ashlar) dressings. The tower has battlements and gargoyles, and the short spire is of limestone. There is a story that when the builders saw the height of Queniborough's spire they gave up and stopped where they were. There is an oddly placed gargoyle in the west wall of the aisle, another on the east wall, and one on each face of the tower, odd in that they do not perform the usual function of gargoyles, that is, to be at the end of a rainwater pipe through which water flows. Perhaps they were from the previous church. There are four gargoyles in the tower, each covered with lead flashing over which rain flows, so these gargoyles again are unusual in that water does not flow through them.

Gargoyle west end south aisle

The gargoyle on the west side of the south aisle is of a gurning face (a grotesque face). On the east side of the south aisle is another gurning face, though this time with the hands on the cheeks instead of in the mouth. On the south of the tower the gargoyle is in the shape of a harnessed bear. The fabric of the chancel seems to be quite early, as does the tower arch, which is probably early twelfth century - which would be if it were transported here. The steeper pitch of the former roof is visible on the outside of the tower wall.

The lower courses of the tower, of Ketton stone, called thus because it was quarried from Ketton in Rutland, also seem to indicate that a more ambitious building was originally planned. But this was abandoned, and the later work is impoverished both in conception and execution. The material was no longer to be the costlier freestone, of which the neighbouring church at Ashby

Folville was contemporaneously built, but a local Waltham ironstone, leaving only the facings of freestone. Although the ironstone has a beauty in its mellow, orange hues, it is porous, and makes it ‘weather’ rather badly, as indeed it has done, although, particularly in the tower, it has withstood this more than might have been expected.

The interior of the church is plain and uncluttered, and in an Early Decorated style. There are plaques in the base of the tower, on the south wall and chancel, and a few tombstones on the floor of the chancel and the nave. The nave roof, which replaced the original, is possibly 15th.century, but the carved wooden shield bearers are 19th.century. The altar rails are simply turned, and are 17th.century. There are two fragments of old stained glass in the east window, and there is a figure of John the Baptist, with his animal skins under the decorated cloak in stained glass by C.E. Kempe in1896. At the west of the church next to the tower there is a blocked up window. This was possibly because of the inability of the village to replace such a large window, or perhaps to give more stability to that wall. The north door, which would have been used by the Lord of the Manor and the priest, is also blocked up, as are the lower halves of the windows in the bell tower. In 1636, after the Reformation, bells were hung in the tower. These have now been taken down because their framework was unsafe, and remain in the tower waiting to be re-hung. The door in the south porch, which is over 100 years old, was made in the village from an oak, which grew in the moat near the church, and was hung in 1885. The only plate of note is a communion cup of 1570.

The large King James’ Bible was a donation from the relatives of the surviving widow of a Rector. The inscription on the inside is: 'Presented by the surviving relatives to South Croxton Church in loving memory of Mrs.Harriet Taylor Wilkinson, a resident of this parish for sixty years, who after a peaceful life of usefulness and charity, died on the 1st.July 1887, having survived her husband, the Reverend John Fernando Wilkinson B.A., late Rector of the parish nearly 20 years.’

From archaeological investigation of the building it can be inferred that the nave and part of the chancel and the tower were the first to be built early in the 14th century. The interior would have been plastered and painted with depictions of events from the bible and of Saints, and the exterior would lave been stuccoed and whitewashed. In the 15th century the chancel was enlarged, the south aisle and porch built, and the whole was re-roofed.

Memorial plaques

In date order:

Mary Barnes (? - 1578) - This is the oldest memorial in the church, and is on the south wall. She died during the reign of Elizabeth I, ten years before the Spanish Armada.

HERE LYETH INTERRED THE BODY OF MARY BARNES
THE DAUGHTER OF RICHARD CHAMBER OF GADDESBY
ESQ.AND WHILE HE LIVED LORD OF HALF THE YOND
BROKE OF THIS TOWN OF SOUTH CROXTON WHICH
MARY HAD ISSUE TWO SONS WILLIAM AND JOHN
AND TWO DAUGHTERS ELIZABETH AND DORCHAS
AND DEPARTED THIS LIFE THE 19TH.FEB.1578

ARAI DALBY – South side, west of the door, slate floor slab:

"Lyeth ye body of
ARAI the wife of
Francis Dalby, who departed this life
An.Domy. 1708
aged 28."

Philip Hackett (1729 -1801) – sanctuary north side, slate floor slab, and chancel north side, slate in wall at ground level.
Left side of slate:
Here lieth the body of Philip Hackett, Rector of this Parish near 31

years. He died March 27th. in the 72nd. Year of his life in the year of Our Lord 1801- 'honoured among men and a friend to the poor'.

Elizabeth Hackett (1742 -1814)
Right side of slate:
Also, at the west end of this stone Elizabeth his widow, who died March 17th 1814, aged 72 years. Her death was occasioned by her clothes taking fire the evening before.

E*H died 1814 – at the base of the north chancel wall, no doubt referring to Elizabeth Hackett, and placed there before the main memorial stone was laid.

Elizabeth Pick (1755-1773) - in the nave of the church, just outside chancel south side, slate floor slab:
Elizabeth Pick, 18 years of age, 1773

Whose life (it's thought) for want of care was lost
Which many sorrowful tears her Parents cost
Their hopes seemed by imprudence (crost)
But trust good God whose wise decrees are best
Has taken her from them to Eternal Rest
And the Celestial Mansions of the Blest.

'A dear and dutiful daughter.'

Mary Taylor Clough (1804 - 1878) - wall plaque in the chancel, white marble on black::
. *'In loving memory of Mary Taylor Clough, who departed this life in full assurance of hope December 4th.1878, age 70 years.'*

Caroline Taylor Clough (1804 - 1884) - wall plaque in the chance, white marble on black:
'In affectionate memory of Catherine Taylor Clough, who from nightly rest was called away into rest eternal, March 26th.1884, aged 80 years.

Blessed are the dead who die in the Lord. Rev.XIV.13
Our loving saviour, Jesus Christ. Titus II.13

Ferdinando Wilkinson (1804 - 1868) – wall plaque in the chancel, white marble on black:

'In affectionate memory of Ferdinando Wilkinson B.A. who departed this life March 22, 1868, aged 64 years, relying solely on the merits and atonement of Jesus Christ, deeply mourned by his bereaved widow, friends and flock. He was Rector of this Parish 40 years, having succeeded his honoured father, the Rev.W.Wilkinson, M.A., whose faithful ministry of 27years in this place has made his name blessed.'

Sarah Ann Adcock (1800 -), daughter of Robert and Mary Adcock. She died soon after her birth and is buried in the choir of the church, on the south side under a choir stall. On her slate slab is:

To the memory of Sarah Ann Adcock
who departed this life in her infancy
the 4th. day of September 1800.
Blessed the dead
Who die in the Lord

Thomas Farmer(1784 - 1836) - south aisle, west end, floor slab of greenish slate:

In memory of Thomas Farmer, who died July the 2nd. 1836, aged 52 years, having been for twenty-four years Clerk of the Parish of South Croxton.
Blessed are the dead who die in the Lord.
Even so, saith the Spirit, for they rest from their labours.

In the base of the tower are three commemorative plaques:

On the left: a plaque bearing four names, probably of Church Wardens –

J.Huskinsson

G.Warden
R.Cross
Plumber
1792

In the centre a plaque commemorating the swift repairs after the lightning strike. It reads:
This tower and spire which were seriously damaged by lightening on June 4th..1936 were restored within the same year.
F.G.Clark Rector
JCK
TF Wardens

On the right, a plaque identical to that on the right, but inscribed –
Ph.Hackett Rector 1792

<u>The History of the Church</u>

By about 800 A.D at the very latest, and probably long before, the Saxons had established a settlement here. It would have been a collection of mud or wooden huts, with water provided by springs and the sinking of wells. There might even have been Celts using the site before that.

Christianity came quietly to these islands with the Romans, though it was proscribed until 312 AD when the Emperor Constantine was converted. When the Romans left, only pockets of Christianity were left, in those places where the Anglo Saxons had not settled. In 579 Pope Gregory sent Augustine to convert them, and within two hundred years of that date this was accomplished. It is likely, therefore, that the first Saxons to live here were already Christian, and had identified their location for worship.

It was common for there to be a cross - known as a 'preaching cross' - on a site which was earmarked for a future church, and that cross was often placed at a spot on which pagan worship had been held, often connected with springs. It is said that there was such a cross in 'Crocheston'. In his 'History of and Antiquities of Leicester' (Vol.III, p.237) Nichols says, "In the church-yard there is the pedeftal of a crofs," and he shows a drawing of such a stump, though whether it was of the one at South Croxton which he saw in 1799 is not clear. Normally such crosses are to the south of a Church, but there is no sign of this cross now. There is what looks like the base of a cross in the Rectory, but it is unlike the engraving, so is unlikely to be that of the original Saxon cross.

Within living memory, the road at Three Turns Lane and outside the Church were widened by the removal of banks. The spoil was dumped on the right of the road to Barsby just as it dips before rising to the village. In it were several large pieces of masonry which by now have disappeared. Could some of these have been the remnants of the preaching cross?

In the reign of William I (the Conqueror), 1 ploughland was held in South Croxton by a foreigner. This foreigner's name was not given in Domesday, but is preserved in the Register of Croxton Abbey, and of Old Malton in Yorkshire as being Adulsus de Brachi, who was a great benefactor to Croxton Abbey, and other churches and convents in England and Normandy. He gave money to build the church of St.John the Baptist at South Croxton, and gave the church a tithe of his revenues from his ploughland. To both Croxton and Old Malton, Adulsus de Brachi, was a liberal benefactor. He gave to Abbeys, including that of Sempringham, some large possessions in Normandy; and in England the church of 'Crokestune', with all its appurtenances; the tenth of all his revenues in Ettuna; and one half of his rent in 'Crokestune'. This church would have been built in the 1080s.

There is likely to have been a church on the site before that, and after the preaching cross was erected. It was probably initially constructed of wood, although pieces of Saxon carved stone have been incorporated into the church, as have some Norman pieces;

perhaps both were from previous builds. We have no direct evidence, but everything points to there being an original, Saxon church, there, perhaps first of wood, and later of stone. Even more telling is its position - on a hilltop, and in a raised churchyard. The road curves round the churchyard, indicating that the churchyard took precedence, either in time or importance. Archaeologists discovered Saxon remains in their dig of 1972, and since the Saxons are known to have occupied existing pagan sites wherever possible, since there is abundant spring water, the origins of South Croxton would seem to be very ancient indeed.

The first mention of a church in South Croxton is in a Croxton Abbey charter between 1196 and 1205, which refers to an earlier document by which Roger de Hotot gave South Croxton church dues and 400 acres of land to the Abbey at Croxton (Kerrial). That was the church built by Adulsus de Brachi, whose name we get from the Register of Croxton Abbey and of Old Malton Abbey, which preceded the present building. It would have been built of stone, with thick walls, small windows. and probably in the early Norman style. It would have been built in a primitive manner, with plain and simple features, perhaps similar in style to the Church of St.Nicholas in Leicester. It would have been an important place for the community to meet. It might have been built in the shape of a 'T', with a nave, a squat tower, and would have been thatched. It would have been stuccoed on the outside and whitewashed.

All the gifts of Adulfus de Brachi were transferred to the Priory at Old Malton (established in about 1150), by the unanimous assent of the monks of Sempringham. Thereafter for about 150 years there was a transfer of the Church, and land, and the right to appoint the priest (advowson) on a number of occasions. The chief beneficiaries of ownership were the nuns of Stamford, the prior and canons of Malton, and for a short period, because South Croxton was so remote and thus of little value, the property was given to the brothers of St.Lazarus at Burton. There was even litigation in the Leicester assizes between Malton Abbey and the nuns of Stamford over rights and ownership.

In 1216 a dispute concerning the church of South Croxton was referred by Pope Innocent III to the Abbots of Kirksteade, Reresby, and Newhous. The Prior and convent of Laund had claimed the church as a chapelry to their church of Ashby Folville; and the Abbot and convent of Croxton (Kerrial) had disputed this.

The area around the church was developed during the early 13th.century, and it was at this time, about 1314, that the present church was built. It was built with thinner walls and more light than the original church. The Norman font was preserved from the previous church, given a new base, and installed in the new church. It is an unusual font; there are 6 large carved pillars to the right of a central figure, and 21 small pillars to the left. Above the small pillars is a top row of interlocking double arches, above the large pillars hoops, from the tops of the pillars. The whole is Norman, except for the curious central figure which dates from a previous time, possibly Celtic.

The church was not an important one, like that at Ashby Folville, for example. So it was built of local ironstone, with ashlar facings. It is likely that bits of the original church were incorporated into the building, like the gargoyles, the pieces of white stone in the porch, and the piece of Saxon carving in the south aisle. The church would have been stuccoed on the outside and painted white, and the interior plastered, and then painted with scenes from scripture and paintings of saints. The last piece of painted plaster was taken down from near the blocked up window in the 1950s for safety reasons. What is certain is that it would have looked very different from the way it looks today.

The possible date of the building of the south aisle, nave roof and chancel of the church is 1450 or earlier, because we know that the roof was replaced 'after a hundred years'.

The Reformation started in 1534 when the official church of the country changed from being Catholic to Protestant. The dissolution of the monasteries started in 1536. We can see that the last Catholic priest could have been Dom Thomas Eyre. 'Dom 'is short for 'Dominus' or 'Lord', and it would be given to a monk who was a Benedictine, a Carthusian or a Cistercian, or else a member of another order who was a Regular Canon, that is, Canons who were in a particular order. (This distinguished them from 'Secular Canons', who were senior diocesan priests, not belonging to an order, but forming a committee to advise the bishop.) So Dom Thomas Eyre could have come from Croxton Abbey, where the Abbott had the patronage of the church in the village. This is the most likely. Or he could have come from Sempringham (1139 - 1558) a Gilbertine order, or from Leicester Abbey (1143 -1538), of the order of St.Augustine. All were 'Canons Regular', and therefore entitled to the title 'Dom'.

Thomas Ayle would have been the first Church of England Minister. He is not given a date, possibly because things at that time, with the disestablishment of the Catholic Church and the dissolution of the monasteries, were in a state of turmoil. The Abbey at Croxton Kerrial was dissolved in 1538. That might have been the date on which Thomas Ayle took up his post At about this time the rood screen would have been removed and destroyed, as well as any statues that might have been in the church.

1578 is the date noted of the death of Mary Barnes on her memorial on the south wall of the church.

In 1636 the bells of the church were hung.
In 1688 South Croxton was one of six parishes in the county to which Richard Woollaston of Wormley in Hereford bequeathed half of two farmhouses and lands in Essex for clothing the poor, to which Frances Holbech in 1737 added £288.5s.for apprenticing two children annually. Richard Woollaston had been in the habit of paying an annual visit to a distant relative at Loseby Hall, and when he did so noticed the 'necessities' of six parishes, which

South Croxton was one. John Nichols tells us that by the late 1700s Philip Hackett realized that there was such an abuse of the charity by the trustees, that the income was reduced to 'a mere trifle'. He convened all the trustees to a meeting in the village. He drew up a document which all signed saying that they would bear equally the cost of putting the charity in order. He searched through the Chancery Rolls and the courts of Doctor's Commons, interviewed everyone concerned, and finally achieved the sum of £15 for each parish, whereas before they received less than £6. The cost to the trustees was no more than £1.5s. each. He would have got more 'if it were not for the mean spiritedness of one or two of his brethren'. It should be noted that the trustees have since been assiduous in looking after the charity, so that a few years ago it was worth £14,000.

The farms whose income was to provide the funds, were adjoining farms, one the Chamberlain's Farm and its land, and the Smith's and Snare's farm and its land, both in Ashingdon, Essex. There was also White House Farm in Letchingdon, Essex. These were known as 'charity estates'.

The same Philip Hackett, the grandson of Philip Hackett who was Rector 1700-1735, almost completely rebuilt the Rectory at his own expense. A silver seal belonging to his grandfather, who had left the village to live in Leicester in 1713, was found in the garden in one of the beds. It had lain there, it was calculated by Rev,Hackett, for 80 years, 'no ways corroded, cankered or blackened."

1773 is the date noted on the memorial slab in the chancel of Elizabeth Pick.

1795-1805 John Nichols published his 'History and Antiquities of the County of Leicestershire' in which South Croxton figures, and from which some of this history of the church derives.
John Nichols' engraving of the church

The Church pews were 'donated' by Rev.Wilkinson, Francis Nedham of Hungarton and George Williamson of Gaddesby in 1810. A legal document in the Leicester Record Office dated 28th.August 1807 specifies the pews or parts of pews allocated to different members of the congregation. It might have been the case that these parishioners paid for the privilege, thus donating the money to purchase the pews, and Messrs Wilkinson, Nedham and Williamson were trustees for the money.

In about 1860 the Rev.Wilkinson built the White House for his sister, and on his death in 1868 his widow moved in with her.

In Wright's Directory of 1898 it was noted that. £800 had been expended upon restoring the church, but further repairs were needed. The leaded windows were removed for a thorough overhaul; the tower parapet was fitted with lead to prevent water seeping through to the tower walls. It was at that time partly covered with ivy, and there is a photograph, discovered in the Rectory, that shows this. A share of the Wollaston charity, producing about £25 a year, was disbursed in clothing.

At the end of the last century, an oak tree growing on the platform of the Moat behind the church was cut down and seasoned for 10 years. Then Bill Glover, a carpenter, with Edward Smith, a wheelwright, made the door that hangs in the south porch. This door was the great pride of Nathanial Glover ('Nat', 1858 -1940), nephew of Bill. Every year from the time it was made, Nat oiled it carefully, and blackened the ironwork.

A copy of the Goscote and Framlingham Deaneries Magazines for 1988 has survived. From it we learn that on 30th August 1889 a sale of work was held in the Rectory, the object of which was to obtain sufficient money to buy an American Organ for the Church.

In October 1899 the following piece appeared: 'Not finding the harmonium of sufficient power and compass for our church a good organ of good tone and compass has been at length procured through the proceeds of a Sale of Work and the money gifts of various kind neighbours and old friends; the moving spirit which elicited so much interest in the musical accompaniment of our devotions was the Organist - many rose to her appeal and the army of workers multiplied to such an extent that ultimately people who had hitherto held aloof also contributed their quota in materials, work or money. This is a healthy symptom and may yet develope (sic) into that plant of tender growth some of us have so earnestly prayed and laboured for – i.e. more unity and effort to understand one another; and so the sale was a very marked success, and many will remember what a pleasant afternoon was spent in and around the Marquee beside the Rectory on August 30th. 1899.

	£	s.	d.
The total expenditure including the cost of the organ*	30	10	4½
Receipts from the sale of work etc.	29	9	0
Deficit	1	1	4½

Mr.Smith-Carrington of Ashby Grange, hearing of our deficiency most generously paid it off and relieved us of all debt.

N.B. It may not be out of place to mention that we are open to receive offers for the purchase of our old harmonium.'
(* .....a contribution towards the cost of the organ, not the total cost)
It is said that the organ came from a house in Bushby.

There follows a piece about the Choir and Congregational outing to Liverpool, where they visited St.Georges Hall, the Museum, and the Britannia S.S, following an 'intelligent and good natured' guide. They had a water trip to New Brighton, and tea before returning to the station at 8p.m., arriving in the village just before dawn.

In about 1900 there was some restoration work undertaken by Rev.F.E.Harwood, rector at that time. A brief account of it was contained in an article of May 2nd.1925. There was then an object bearing the arms of Thomas de Bretherton, Earl of Norfolk (15th.century), which used to be preserved on the north wall of the church. There might be a drawing of it somewhere, according to the article. There also used to be a loose glass panel, hanging on the east window of the chancel, and bearing the arms of Beaumont. There used to be heraldic paintings over the arches of the tower, and the south of the nave, more recently removed because of the unsatisfactory condition of the plaster. These are noted by Burton (1622) and the 1900 'Leicester Advertiser' article.

A major reconstruction of the Church had to take place in 1925, again described in the same article. The masonry of the whole body of the church seems to have been defective, and the foundation work unstable, and the thrust of the arches became too great for the structure. The North wall had separated from the tower and the whole wall bowed outwards. The rest was in an unsatisfactory condition. Thus, in 1925 work was carried out to rectify this by Mr.W.Agar of Syston, under the architect, Mr.Grundy of Leicester. At that time evidence was unearthed of the design of a north aisle, apparently abandoned, and a wall almost flush with the tower wall took its place.

In the Leicestershire Record Office there is a document itemising the work to be done, and a plan of the church with changes highlighted. The document itemises:

1. Underpin and shore up SE of south wall. Take down and rebuild the pier which was out of vertical.

Underpin north wall of the church and bond the piers to the main wall.

3. Construct a drainage channel round the church.

Insert louvers and wire netting in the spire and tower, construct doors at the head of the stairs, point up where necessary.

5. Repair the roof spouting and walls generally.

6. Remove fillings from west corner of the south aisle; repair the mullions and reglaze.
Remove and destroy wood block flooring and pews which were infected by dry rot, and lay composition flooring on the existing concrete foundation; supply new seating and repair the floor where necessary.
8. To strip internal walls of the nave and south aisle of the plaster and lime wash, and point up and insert new stones where necessary.
To move the organ from the north side of the nave, and re-erect it on a low platform on the South side.
To supply a new base to the existing top part of the pulpit, and re-erect the pulpit on the north side of the nave in the space vacated by the organ.
To place a new top on the Holy Table to increase its length to 6 feet, and add Riddel posts and curtains.
To remove the existing two stone steps upon which the Holy Table stands, and move the communion rail and step about 4 feet forward.
To move the three seats at the eastern end of the south aisle to the north side of the nave, and hang a curtain at the back of the organ.
The work would cost £1,100, and there was £160 in hand. The work would be done as money became available.

It is interesting to note that the plan of the church shows the font in a more or less central position at the back of the church, and not well to the south as it is at present.

Bob Parker installed the first electricity supply to the Church in 1936. He had one of the first cars in the village, and ran a garage opposite and just further up from the Church.

The Clarion reported in the autumn of 1969 that a seat dedicated to the memory of Mrs.Una Clark, wife of the Reverend Frederick George Clark, Rector 1934 -1959, had been stolen from the Church Yard, and a tombstone smashed.

On June 4th.1936 the tower was struck by lightning, and the southeast corned of the tower was demolished. A great deal of damage was done to the roof where masonry had crashed through, just missing the ancient font. The Rector at the time, Rev.F.G.Clarke, gives this description:

"I happened to be looking at the church out of the window during the storm. The flash of lightening seemed to envelop the church. The whole building appeared as if it were surrounded by flames. When the flash disappeared I saw what looked like smoke rising upwards, and when that cleared I saw that the top of the steeple and part of the tower had disappeared. I rushed across to the church, and found that stonework had smashed through the church and was piled up on the floor."

Appeals were made for funds to supplement the settlement by the Ecclesiastical Insurance Office. The reason for this, as evidenced by the appeals, was not only to repair the substantial damage, but also to remedy the damage caused by death watch beetle, and general decay of the woodwork that was discovered.

The following letter was published as an appeal for funds for the restoration of the church fabric:

APPEAL LETTER

DIOCESE OF LEICESTER
Dated July 1937.

On Thursday, 4th. June, 1936, a disastrous storm broke over, and caused great havoc to our church. The tower and the spire were struck by lightning and great masses of stone crashed through the roofs of the nave and south aisle, extensively damaging them, and the interior of the church. Serious damage was also done to the church furniture, window tracery and glass, and other items, repairs and renewals of which have to be faced.

The Ecclesiastical Insurance Office has been very generous for which we are most grateful, and our parishioners have also raised the sum of £110 during the past year towards the cost of restoration. This is very creditable in view of the small and diminishing population of the village.

Our financial resources are, however, very limited, and although many others have come to our help, we are obliged to appeal for further support. The work of restoration is almost finished, but another £500 is sorely needed if we are to complete it.
May we ask for your help? The sympathy already shown to us, and the love for our old and beautiful churches, assures us we shall not appeal in vain.

Any donation will be gratefully received and acknowledged.
F.G. Clark (Rector).
T.N. Fairbrother (Churchwarden).
J.I. Knapp (Church warden).

<u>LETTER FROM THE LORD BISHOP OF LEICESTER</u>.

BISHOP'S HOUSE,

LEICESTEB.

5th.May,1937

The extensive injury by lightning to South Croxton church was a great tragedy. Unhappily the amount required for its restoration is not fully covered by the insurance. The people in the parish are giving well, but help is needed from friends outside it if the total amount required is to be raised. I shall be very grateful to any who feel able to assist.

(Sgd.) Cyril, Leicester.

LETTER FROM THE RURAL DEAN.

I warmly endorse this appeal. South Croxton is only a tiny place. I have both helped them myself, and appealed to neighbouring parishes with some success. But further help is sorely needed.

G.E. BRITTEN
Rural Dean Goscote 1.

LETTER FROM THE ARCHITECT

Friar Lane, Leicester.
This is one of those unfortunate instances where the damage occasioned by the storm has revealed other troubles. The Insurance Office concerned has been generous in the matter of restoration of the fabric. Other defects have, however, been brought to light, such as extensive ravages by the Death-Watch Beetle and general decay of woodwork; these have required immediate attention, thereby involving increased work and expense.

The work so far carried out presented much danger and risk to the workmen, but fortunately no mishap has occurred.

Albert Herbert, F.R.I., B.A., F.S.A.

The damage to the spire was made good in the same year, and a plaque in the bell tower commemorates this achievement. Other restoration work was carried out over the next two years

A newspaper cutting of November 2nd.1938 reads:

"RESTORED CHURCH SPIRE FLOODLIT - THANKSGIVING SERVICE AT SOUTH CROXTON

Only a little more than two years after the spire and tower of South Croxton church were struck by lightning, a service of thanksgiving for the completion of restoration work was conducted at the church last night by the Bishop of Leicester, assisted by the Archdeacon of Leicester and the Rural Dean, Canon G.E. Britten.

In celebration of the occasion the church spire was floodlit, and provided a magnificent spectacle over the surrounding countryside.

The Bishop expressed his pleasure at being able to take part in so happy a ceremony and thanked all who, by gifts and work, had helped in the completion, at a cost of £2,300, of the very heavy task.
He mentioned that an anonymous contribution of £50 had that evening been received toward the outstanding cost.

The Rector of South Croxton, the Rev. F.G. Clarke, also acknowledged his gratitude to friends in all parts of the country who had willingly and sympathetically helped the parish in its need. During the service the Bishop also dedicated the electric lighting, which has recently been installed in the church.

Among those present at the service were Major and Mrs. Burnaby, Sir Harold and Lady Nutting, and visiting clergy from Queniborough, Twyford, Beeby and Ashby Folville.

The evening concluded with an entertainment given at the village hall by a Leicester concert party."

Outside the south door there is a stone memorial surmounted by a lamp, and donated by the Sunday School to commemorate this work. The inscription reads:
This lamp was presented by the Sunday School Scholars in gratitude for the restoration of the church during the years 1936-1938

According to the Rev.Priston, in the 1950s the last piece of mediaeval painted plaster was removed from near the blocked window in the west wall for safety reasons.

A piece from the Mercury of 9th.January 1962 says that although the Rector, Rev.Ian Phelps was hesitant to spend money on floodlighting when the church needed so many repairs, so many offers of money had come forward, that a do-it-yourself scheme, with materials obtained at a discount, with an estimated cost of £79 to £100 could be reached.

Various maintenance and repair work was carried out to the church in 1970 by a Leicester building firm of which two directors, George and Simon Duxbury, lived in the village. (George was the father of Julian Duxbury, co-publisher of, and contributor to this book.) The work included repairs to the pews and the installation of wall-mounted candle holders. Their major project took place when a bolt from the bell frame fell down the tower to the church floor. This caused great concern about the safety of the bells, and it was decided that they should be taken down. Duxbury's constructed a platform in the tower, and then cut through the old oak frame to lower the bells onto it. Because of the strength and thickness of the frame the work took over a week. One of the workmen, Roy Springthorpe, shaped a cross from a piece of bell iron, and carved an angel from the oak frame.

Figure made from bell frame.

The cross stands on the altar when it is thought wise to replace the silver one, and the angel stands in a recess in the north aisle.

Cross made from bell hanging.

A piece from the Leicester Mercury of 10th.December 1958 says that while repairs to the lightning rod were being carried out (frost had made it come away from the stonework) it was discovered that holes had been shot in the weather vane shaped like a cockerel. The Rector, Rev.F.Clark, says it was believed to be the work of people out shooting pigeons. The repairs would cost about £20, which would reduce the money available for necessary repairs.
In order to cut costs, the original Old Rectory was sold in 1981, and a new and smaller one built in its place.

Like many churches, South Croxton had been finding it difficult to pay its way, and to pay for the upkeep of the Church. The Diocese of Leicester had come up with the idea of Parish Planned Funding throughout the diocese. This started in the village in 1995, and continued renewing itself every four years. This entailed villagers being asked to make a monthly contribution to the Church, whether they were churchgoers or not. Thus those who appreciated the sociological and historical importance of the Church building were able to contribute to it, and the scheme enabled the Church to receive tax relief on everybody's contributions.

It was sadly a sign of the times that the Church, which had been opened throughout the day, had to be locked unless there were someone present. The visitors' book used to contain entries of appreciation for the open Church, but when Jim Bishop, who lived in the barn conversions near the Church, resigned as Church Warden in 1995, there was no one to keep an eye open for visitors, so it had to be kept locked. However, it was kept open from Christmas 2004 to see what would happen. Nothing did, so still in August 2005 it remains open. The only problem is that if the door is left open, house martins get in and cannot escape. So the porch light and the light on the Sunday School Memorial is left on so that they can be guided out on dark evenings should any enter. A small orchestra performed at the 2002 Arts Festival, and I had to apologise publicly to them for playing something in C major, while the martins chirped away in D flat.

The floodlights first installed in 1938, and then renewed in 1962, but which had not worked for some time, were renovated, and parts replaced in time for the Millennium. They were switched on at Christmas Eve 1999, and the church was lit each night from then.

Stump of Saxon Preaching Cross by Nochols

10 Archaeology of the Church

Dr Graham Jones, Lecturer in English Topography and Research Fellow at the University of Leicester Centre for English Local History, was invited by the author to visit the village, and especially the Church, on August 12th.2003. We toured the churchyard, and he noted that it was large, and oblong shaped, conforming (as does the curtilage of the North Manor) with the rectilinear area defined by the two roads running north from the village and containing also the moated site. He noted that the ground fell away sharply at the southeast corner of the yard into an overgrown area and wondered if this had been the location of a spring. We exited by the gate opposite the Old Rectory and went uphill to the Moated Site. He thought that the moat might have been constructed as much for the fish with which it was stocked as for protection of the platform it surrounds. We noted that the church was a little downhill from that site. There were springs there, at least one feeding the moat. He noted the ditch, which bordered the road by the Moated Site, and continued behind the hedge, which bordered the churchyard in a straight line.

We returned to the churchyard and looked at the original roofline on the tower wall. (See the illustration ay the beginning of the chapter on The Church.) He noted that It was typical of rooflines of the 13th and 14th centuries. We saw that it covered only the nave. This we thought suggested that the south aisle had been built later than the nave, and that the aisle was a 15th.century addition, contemporaneous with the wooden roof inside. He looked at the south wall, and noted that a whitish-coloured moulding which had run from the porch suddenly stopped, and later there was another, of a different stone and type running along, round the rounded door, and continuing along the chancel wall. He noted that the windows were in two pairs, the two inner, and the outer pair. We looked at the east end and the north wall. He noted the windows, only two of which matched, and the rib of a possible arch in the wall by the tower. We noted too a Norman door into the chancel, quite out of keeping with the rest of the church. This too we thought might have come from a previous build.

Norman door in the chancel

We went round the west end, and he noted the gargoyle which served no useful purpose, on the west wall, but matches that on the east wall. Looking up and seeing the gargoyles around the top of the tower, he thought these were of similar design and wondered if the south aisle gargoyles had been deliberately preserved from a previous 'build' and reset for display and perhaps for symbolism.

When we turned our attention to the porch he immediately noted a large, whitish stone with a channel cut into it on its left, and what

Piece of a possible stone panel, left of the porch.

might have been carving on its right. We went round to the other side of the porch and found a similar stone, partly covered by the drainpipe. They obviously come from the same piece, possibly from a tomb cover or some other carved panel, and he wondered if they might have been deliberately incorporated into the walls of the porch.

Inside the porch on the right of the west wall was a curious stone, which had a hole in the middle, and lines radiating outwards, a Mass Dial. (There are about 3000 of these in the country, and this one has now been registered with the Mass Dial Society.)

Mass Dial in the porch.

A Mass Dial is usually situated on the outside of the south porch, so this one has obviously been relocated. There is a white stone on the front of the porch where it might have previously been placed. It was used in the days before clocks and watches to denote the times of services. On entering the church he was amazed and delighted by the font. It was from about 1100AD, was Norman, and had an upper row of interlacing circles,

Font figure.

6 to the left and 21 smaller ones to the right, springing from a bottom row of pillars. It has a curious central figure. While the pillars and arches are early Norman, the figure is remarkably like a Celtic one.

He noted the massive tower arch, which dated from the 12th. century and predated the church, and on the west side he noted that the masonry blocks had not been shaped, but had mortar infill where they met the rounded arch. He noted the rib of a possible arch from the tower, and the filled in door He noted that it was high, which to him denoted processions and the carrying of crosses and banners. On the north wall he noted a number of large stones, as elsewhere in the structure. That indicated either a sudden input of wealth, or stones which had been imported with the other bits like the windows and tower arch, and incorporated into the smaller ironstone pieces which made up the remainder of the walls. There were several of these partial rows of stones about the church, as well as individual stones inset among the ironstone material. (The wall had been rebuilt in 1925 and possibly in 1936, so the stones were not necessarily in their original places.)

He noted that there was no evidence of a rood screen which must have been there, so it had possibly been situated in front of the chancel arch. He noted a plaster infill to the right of the arch, which sounded hollow, and which we thought might have been the entrance to the steps which would have led to the rood screen loft. As it is raised from the floor we thought that external steps would have led to it.

On the north wall of the chancel in front of the altar, he noted a vertical row of large stones, and matching it on the other wall what might have been a line denoting a join. This might suggest that the end of the chancel was built later than the main body of the church, perhaps contemporaneously with the south aisle and the roof. Indeed, Pesvner says that the south aisle and chancel extension were built later than the nave. He noted the rounded door on the south wall, and we thought that it did not quite fit in, because the remainder of the church is in Early Decorated style. So it too might have been an oddment from another building, or even one that had been salvaged from the previous Norman church. He noted mason's marks in a stone on the right of the door.

When we turned our attention to the south aisle, his attention was immediately caught by a piece of whitish stone high on the east wall. He was as excited by this as by the font. He noted that it appeared to be a fragment of a larger carved panel, showing costume folds, most likely belonging to the robe of a

Saxon carving

Male person (possibly clerical vestments, or the robe of a biblical character). He noted that the location of the panel is highly suggestive, being on the north side of the former aisle altar, the position reserved in medieval churches for the image of the patron saint of the altar.

The Church in winter 2000

11 The Church Bells of South Croxton

Church bells on their platform in the tower

John Nichols (History and Antiquities of Leicester Vol.p.236) says that these bells 'are pretty tunable songsters, cast by the same hands that cast St.Margaret's ancient six, the celebrated Mr.Watts, as appears by his signature.

Hugh Watts (who was born, as we gather from his epitaph, about the year 1582) was about eighteen years of age at his father's death. He placed his name, as founder, in the same year, upon a bell at Burrow-on-the-Hill, in this county, since recast:

'Hugh Wattes made me 1600,'

and upon the present second bell at Evington is a similar inscription, dated 1605. These are the only instances that have been found in which he followed the custom so soon prevalent with all founders of putting their names on the bells they cast. Upon this Evington bell is the shield here given:

"Hugh Watts soon obtained a high reputation as a founder; his are still extremely numerous in Leicestershire - there are nearly two hundred of them - where they are noted for the beauty and fullness of their tone. Several complete rings are to be found; as at Asfordby, South Croxton, Whitwick, Arnesby and Thorpe Langton."

SOUTH CROXTON

S.John the Baptist 4 bells

1. GOD (9) SAVE (9) THE (9) kING(sic) (9) 1636
   (On all the bells the inscription is followed by the shield above P.S.)
   (Diam.26 1/2")

2. IHS: NAZARENVS (9) REX: IVDEORUM (9) FILI DEI (9) MISERERE: MEI (9) 1636
   (Note - the 'S' in IH'S is inscribed backwards. PS)

3. The same. (Diam. 32 1/2")

4. The same, dated 1637. (Diam.35")

At the death knell three tolls are given for a male, two for a female, both before and after the knell.'

Taken from: The Church Bells of Leicestershire: their inscriptions, traditions and peculiar uses; with chapters on bells and the Leicester bell founders
by Thomas North,
Honorary Secretary of the Leicestershire Architectural and Archaeological Society, and Member of the Royal Archaeological Institute of Great Britain and Ireland,
with illustrations.
Published in Leicester: by Samuel Clarke, 1876

The bells are lying on a platform in the spire of the church, and there is a fund to restore them. According to Ecclesiastical Law, if the bells are in the church, they may not be replaced by electronic bells.

Old Rectory

12 THE CHURCH OF ST JOHN THE BAPTIST, SOUTH CROXTON

LIST OF KNOWN RECTORS

	Date	Years served
Thomas de Northampton	1187	36
John de Salteby	1223/4	40
John de Graham	1263/4	26
Robert de Strathirne	1289	7
Geofforey de Somerdby	1296	18
William de Stoketh	1313/4	35
John Nicholas de Howes	1349	10
Henry Mye	1359	21
Dom Ralph	?	?
Richard Mathew	1380	?
Dom Robert Wytrych	?	?
Stephen de Tybbey	1413	1
Dom John Mason	1414/5	?
Dom William Stodman	?	?
Robert Seleby	1441	30
Dom William Stevynson	1471	4
Henry Sherard	1475/6	8
Dom Anthony Mallery	1483/4	8
William Tagge	1491	5
Dom Seth Attyrchyff	1496	5
Helyas Atturchyff	1501	25
Dom Thomas Bennet	1526	6
Dom Thomas Eyre	1532	?
Thomas Ayle	?	?
Edmund Willock	1576	4

Hugh Osborne	1580	3
William Kaye	1583	16
Thomas Rest	1609	32
Robert Bridges	1647	15
Paul Balgay	1662	28
Thomas Sawbridge	1690	10
Philip Hackett	1700	35
William Middleton	1735	30
Robert Burnaby	1765	5
Phillip Hackett	1770	31
William Wilkinson	1801	13
William Wilkinson	1814	14
John Fernando Wilkinson	1828	40
Humphry Noble	1868	25
Francis Edward Harwood	1893	16
John Wallace Watts	1919	4
Dudley Gibson Bishop	1923	3
Llewellyn Wynn Watkins	1926	8
Frederick George Clarke	1934	25
Ian James Phelps	1959	9
Robert Beresford Capron	1968	3
David Leslie Priston	1971	23
Malcolm Lambert	1994	6
Derek Dolman	2000	6

13 Echoes in the Churchyard

AT THE GOING DOWN OF THE SUN

On the south side of' the churchyard, at the edge of' the path that leads to the south door, is a stone memorial to the men of' South Croxton who were killed in action during the Great War 1914 - 1918. It is significant that from such a small village six lives were lost.

The inscription reads:

THIS CROSS IS ERECTED AND PRESENTED AS A TOKEN OF LOVE AND GRATITUDE AND IN GRATEFUL MEMORY OF THE COURAGE AND DEVOTION OF OUR VALIANT DEAD

Cecil A. Hunt

Albert Dukes

Fred W. East

George Adams

Sam Adams

Fred Sharpe

CECIL A. HUNT (1883 - 1916)

Cecil was born in South Croxton in 1893, the son of' William and Elizabeth Hunt. He joined the Royal Engineers when the Great War began, in 1914. He was killed on November 13, 1916, at the age of' 23 years. He was killed in France, but his body was brought back to England for burial in South Croxton. Cecil was laid to rest in the northern section of' the churchyard, and his mother and father, when they came to die, were laid in the same grave.

ALBERT DILKES (? -1917)

Albert was born in South Croxton, was killed in France in 1917. He was a sergeant. His body was buried in France.

FRED W. EAST (? - 1917)

Fred was born in South Croxton, and was a private soldier. He was killed in France on October 20, 1917, and was buried there.

GEORGE ADAMS (? - 1918)

George was born in South Croxton. He was a Colonel in the army, and he was killed in France in the last weeks of' the Great War.

SAM ADAMS (? - 1917)

Sam was the brother of Colonel George Adams, and was killed in France in 1917, some months before his brother.

FRED SHARPE (? - 1918)

Fred was born in South Croxton, and was an army private. He was killed in France in the last year of' the Great War.

Some of the lettering has worn over the years, and is difficult to read.

The Churchyard

Very few memorials in churchyards date before the end of the 17th.century. Before that graves were unmarked, except for the very rich or important who often had memorials in the church. There were no coffins except those for the very rich, and bodies were wrapped in a cloth or blanket to be buried. So we are limited in our research in the graveyard to those memorials standing now.

In the past many families lived in the village for hundreds of years.

Then came the Industrial Revolution which started in the villages. When that phase was over, many villagers had moved to town to seek the sort of work they had been doing. For this reason many families who had been in the village for many generations seem to disappear.

The Huskinson graves

The Huskinson family had been prominent in South Croxton for over 150 years. The gravestones date from 1792 to 1811 are in a family plot to the west of the churchyard.

Samuel Huskinson - 1732-1792, aged 60. In the tower is a memorial plaque to him, as church warden and bell ringer.
Joice Huskinson – 1736-1816, wife of Samuel, aged 80, survived her husband 26 years.
John Huskinson – 1764-1843, aged 79. Probably unmarried.
Thomas Huskinson – 1775-1817, aged 42. died 9 months after his mother.
Elizabeth Huskinson – 1763-1853, wife of Thomas, aged 90. She was 12 years older than her husband.
Joseph Huskinson, son of Samuel and Joice, has no gravestone, but is mentioned on the gravestone of his two sons.
Mary Huskinson, wife of Joseph, has no gravestone, but is mentioned on the gravestone of her two sons.
Joseph Huskinson (1807-1811) and John Huskinson (1809-1811) rest in the same grave, Joseph died at 4, John at 2.

The Talbot graves

The Talbot graves lie in the north of the graveyard. From the birth of the first to the death of the last covers 200 years.

William Talbot – no extant memorial, but is mentioned on the grave of his son, David.
Hannah Talbot – no extant memorial, but is mentioned on the grave of her son, David.

David Talbot (1780-1853) aged 73, son of William and Hannah.

The Holyland Graves

The Holyland graves are situated in the western section of the churchyard, and the plot holds just three gravestones.

1. William Holyland, died 1857, age *59* years.
2. William Holyland, died 1864, age 88 years.
   Susanna Holyland, died 1862, age 65 years, daughter of William Holyland Senior.
   Amy Simpson, died in 864, age 70 years, daughter of William Holyland Senior
3. Mary Hoyland, died 1827, age 61 years, wife of Will Holyland, Senior.

WILLIAM HOLYLAND (1776 - 1864).
William married very young, and his wife, Mary, was 10 years older than him, born in 1766. When did he marry? His daughter, Amy, was born in 1794, so he must have married Mary at 18 years old or less.
They had a daughter, Amy, a son, William, was born in 1798, and another daughter, Susanna, was born in 1799.

William and Mary were married for more than 30 years, and we know that Mary suffered for a long time from poor health. She died in 1827, at the age of 61 years

William lived on for another 37 years. His daughter, Amy, was married into the Simpson family. The younger daughter, Susanna, never married.

The son, William, at the age of' 59, in 1857, was probably murdered. He was unmarried.
William Holyland died on February 7, 1864, at the age of 88 years.

MARY HOLYLAND (1766 – 1827)
Mary Holyland was the wife of' William Holyland, Senior. Her memorial stone states that she died ìafter a series of sufferings. Mary died on January 9, 1827, at the age of 61 years.

SUSSANNA HOLYLAND (1799 – 1862)
Susanna Holyland was the daughter of William and Mary Holyland. She remained unmarried and lived all her life in the house of her father. She died 2 years before her father, on February 2, 1862, at the age of 63 years. She shares a grave with her father and sister, Amy.

AMY SIMPSON (nee Holyland). (1794 - 1864)
Amy Simpson was the daughter of William and Mary Holyland. Amy was married to one of the Simpsons. She died just 7 months after her father, on September 10, 1864, at the age of 70 years. She shares a grave with her father and sister.

WILLIAM HOLYLAND, JUNIOR.
William Holyland was the son of William and Mary Holyland. He was probably unmarried. He died on August i6, 1837, at the age of 59 years. The inscription on his grave reads:

TYRANTS DID RISE UP AGAINST ME
AND THRUST SORELY AT ME WITHOUT CAUSE
BUT MY HOPE IS IN THEE, OH GOD,
WHO WILL AVENGE THE BLOODTHIRSTY MAN.

It is therefore possible that William was murdered.

This section is based on notes made by Roy King in 1980.

Nave of the Church and tower arch

14 Methodism

The village was a Methodist stronghold in the latter half of the nineteenth century and into the early part of the twentieth. In 1869 a Primitive Methodist chapel was built behind the Golden Fleece, and 'Kings Lane' became 'Chapel Lane'. This was part of the Melton Mowbray and Oakham Primitive Methodist Circuit. According to the minutes of the trustees, the chapel was 9 yards long (later reduced to 8 yards) built of brick with a Bangor slate roof, had four metal windows and a fanlight over the door, and gable ends. Because it was built on a bank there were steps leading up to it, and Sybil Barsby remembers nine. It contained a single room which could hold 50 people, lit by two chandeliers each with 5 lamps, and furnished with six pews, 2'6" wide. There were wrought iron gates at the entrance to the Chapel yard. The inscription over the door read, 'Primitive Methodist Provident Chapel 1856.'. It was built by a Mr.Groves for £136.10s.0d. To date there are no photographs of it.

There is, however, a previous mention of Methodism in South Croxton found in the House of Lords Proceedings, Vol.63 1830 dated 16 November 1830:
'Petition received from members of a society and Congregation of Wesleyan Methodists worshiping at Barsby and South Croxton chapels.'
The petition was one of many received from around the country supporting the abolition of slavery in the colonies and dominions.

By 1943 the Chapel had become dilapidated, and was in an 'appalling state'. It had not been used for some years, and services were held in the Village Hall which was rented at a very reasonable rate. The cost of repairs, including the buttressing of the walls, would be £200, and £20 for redecoration. By 1947 a decision was made to sell the Chapel and put the proceeds into an account for 're-establishing the cause' in the village. In 1948 Mr.Eagles of Melton had tried to work up the cause by concentrating on the village for 6 months. This was to no avail, and a final decision to sell was made in 1950. At the last meeting of the trustees it was noted that the Village Hall was no longer rented because of the drop in numbers attending. There was certain property lodged in the Hall which belonged to the Chapel, like an inscribed table, hymn books and bibles, and these were disposed of. There was a balance in the accounts of £18 17s.4d. plus money from the sale of the building which was disbursed among Methodist building schemes and causes. In 1951 the chapel was sold for £35 and pulled down. Later the area was included in a car park for the Golden Fleece. The name 'Chapel Lane' reverted to 'Kings Lane'.

There are two references in the Minutes of the School Board that might indicate the convictions of the Methodists.

The first is in a minute of July 1906. It noted that the Rector attended the school most mornings for bible readings and explanations. They wondered if this was legal. If not, the Rector, at that time the Rev.Francis Harwood, should be asked to discontinue the practice. They must have enquired of the County Council, because there was a reply on August 2nd.1906 saying that it was up to the managers, and they voted, 3 for 2 against, letting the Rector continue. Subsection 2 of section 14 of the Education Act of 1870 said that no religious catechism or formulary which is distinctive of any particular denomination should be taught in the school. They were largely of the opinion that his teaching did not infringe that section.

The second is in a minute of January 20th.1910, which notes that Mr.J.Swift resigned from the Board because he could not agree that the school should be used for whist drives and dances.

15 The School

The school with the policeman – undated, about 1900

The school at South Croxton in School Lane was built in 1884 to hold 60 children. According to an inscription on a brick on the side of the building, the builder was Mr.Middleton of Leicester.

In 1870 the Education Bill gave religious and voluntary bodies a year's grace to build schools across the country. After that the various School Boards which had been created nation-wide would step in to fill the gaps. These gaps existed mainly in rural areas, and the school at South Croxton would have been part of the gap filling. A minute of October 1907 said that the villagers had contributed towards the cost of the building, but this would have been unusual; the Board of Education in London would have paid for the building and its equipment from central funds. It might have been that the village contributed to extra items, much as Parent-Teacher Associations do now. The addition of a second 'public' building after over 800 years must have been a momentous event.

There was some form of education before 1884. There are teachers noted in the Directories who would have taught from their homes - or even the Rectory. One was a governess and then became a teacher. Children would probably have paid a penny a week. Other provision would have been within families where children received rudimentary instruction in their letters and how to count, and perhaps sewing for the girls. There might have been a Dame school where a local woman would have taught children, usually in their kitchen. The better off villagers would have probably sent their children as boarders to Leicester, Loughborough, or even further afield. All this must remain supposition until evidence is uncovered. Wright's Directory for 1863 notes that Ann Morley was the schoolmistress, and Ann Randell the Infants teacher, though where the school was is unclear.

At least one Rector held classes in the Rectory: ''Ambrose goes to a private school in South Croxton kept by the Rev.W.Wilkinson.' ("Information on Wilkinson" by E.S.Purcell 2 vols.) Ambrose would have had to make the daily journey from Loughborough, so the school must have been a particularly good one, or the Rev.Wilkinson might have had good connections.

Another reference to the same school in South Croxton is in 'The Catholic Encyclopaedia':
'From 1818 (when he was nine) to 1820 Ambrose Phillips of Garendon Park, Loughborough attended a private school in South Croxton run by Rev.Wilkinson. When aged 16 and attending a Protestant school lin Birmingham he converted to Catholicism and had to leave the school. He returned to the private tuition of Rev.Wilkinson to prepare for his entry to Cambridge University.
Ambrose Phillips later retook the old family name of de Lisle and dedicated himself to Catholic causes and scholarship.' He rebuilt Grace Dieu Manor partly with the famous architect A.W.Pugin, and founded The Cistercian monastery at Mount St.Bernard Abbey.' The De Lisle Comprehensive School in Loughborough is named after him.

School group, early 1900s.

Although the school opened in 1884, there are only three records prior to 1904. These are reports of His Majesty's Inspectors, and the grants payable from central funds as a result of them. These reports were in a box that was carried out of the school in early 1968 by a workman whose job it was, it is supposed, to 'clear the school'. Mrs.Maude Nicol, who lived next to the school, asked him what he was going to do with them, and he replied, "Put them on that bonfire." She took them off him, and are in her possession. They are reproduced at the end of this chapter. The log books, punishment books and all other documents that were in the school are lost. The managers' Minutes from 1884-1907 are not to be found in County Hall or in the Records Office.

The Managers' minutes from 1907 lodged in the Leicestershire Records Office in Wigston are very sketchy. Very few names of children or of teachers are to be found before about 1940. In 1899, Kelley's Directory notes that the Schoolmistress was Jane Smith, and the Infants teacher Florence Screaton.

Although the school was built for 60 pupils it was never full. The highest number was 51 (1907), and the lowest 7 (1954). For most of this century it was less than half full.
In July 1906 there were galleries in the Infant Department, and it

was arranged that the chairman, Mr.J.Smith, who was also a carpenter, should remove them. There was also a trapdoor there.

The following are excerpts from the minutes:

School number: 205; registration number: 21/205/3.

21.11.04
Proposed extension to and repair of playground.

19.4.05
Miss F.M.Screaton, a Supplementary Teacher(1), applied for an increase in salary. She was 26 yrs.old,had been appointed in 1899, received £20 p.a. which was less than others in the area.

19.4.05
The Education Committee was to supply one teacher's desk and stool, 2 scholars' desks no.2, length 8', height 2'6" and seats Height 18"

2.1.06
Miss Screaton's application was denied.

26.7.09
An Inspector, Mr Lott, visited and found that the children read with some fluency, but that few of the older children had acquired a taste for reading. Written work, arithmetic and composition were weak.
Possibly as a consequence of this report, in April 1909 it was noted that it was not necessary to retain the services of Miss Ada Hamson, an Uncertificated Teacher(2), at her present salary, and recommended that the Education Department give her a month's notice and advertise for a Supplementary Teacher.

Emma Smith was Head Teacher.
20.1.10

Mr.J.Swift resigned from the Board of Managers because he could not agree with the use of the school hall for Whist Drives and Dances. (This was a Methodist stronghold.) Mr.G.Black was elected in his place.

11.5.10
Visit of the Inspector, Mr.Lott:
“Considering the isolated position of the village and the scant opportunity the children have of acquiring experience and vocabulary outside their own immediate surroundings, the general condition of the children is very creditable to the teacher.”

3.10.10
Miss Kate Pollard was appointed as Supplementary Teacher.

29.6.14 HMI
Miss F.A.Jones inspected.
‘the work has been prepared with praiseworthy intent to cultivate originality. The children are on the whole intelligent and responsive, and very friendly relations exist between them and their teachers.’

25.1.15
Miss Pollard was promoted to Headmistress.

11.2.15
Miss Pollard’s salary was increased by £2.10s. p.a.

27.3.15
Board of Education grant of £96 for the previous year.

28.4.16
The services of Miss Pollard were to be retained as 8 more children could be entering the school, and a suitable monitress(3) could be sought.
11.5.17 31 on roll, + 5 more soon.

4.6.19
HMI Mr.A.T.Kerslake
'Progress has been affected in recent years through epidemics and migration of families, but is now better. Their plots in the playground show their interest in gardening.'

24.10.19
Increase of £5 a year salary to Miss Pollard. This is applicable to all certificated teachers in the County, now being £182.10s.p.a. 29 on roll.

34 on roll.
Supplementary Teacher was not needed, but could seek a full time monitress to teach the youngers.

5.12.21
The Headmistress was allowed to attend meetings of the Board.

20.4.22
'The Monitress has been subjected to treatment from a villager that would prove detrimental to the Monitress's influence in the school. It was decided to send a letter of warning to the villager.'

18.10.22
The school is characterised by an excellent tone, very good discipline and quiet and effective teaching. (Assumed to be a report of 2 managers who periodically visited the school.)

28.5.23
Gladys Knapp to be appointed a pupil teacher(4) in place of Janet Amos, resigned.

25.5.25
6 dual desks were to be ordered to replace the long, worn ones. The clock to be repaired. There was to be an additional member of staff, and 2 high teachers' chairs.

21.1.26
There were a number of complaints about the state of the playground.
A complaint had been received from a villager about the Headmistress. Resolved the matter be left on the table.

13.2.28
The Headmistress, Mrs.Harrison to take 7 weeks rest for her health.
An Assistant Teacher provided because of ill health of both teachers and epidemic illness.
In the near future it was expected that the school would be decapitated by the Seniors going to Barsby School. The Headmistress would be able to manage on her own.

The Correspondent was to write to the Headmistress with regard to low attendance, and also with reference to the children in school not being clean.

11.5.31
Miss Harrison resigned to take up a Headship in Lincolnshire.

15.6.31
There were 12 applications for Head Teacher, 3 were to be interviewed. Miss L.M.Burrell of Nuneaton appointed.
HMI Kerslake noted that the new head had made a 'promising commencement'.

Miss Burrell and Miss Coggan with the school 1933.

17.9.34
Joan Coggan, pupil teacher(4), had left in July 1934, and had not been replaced because of low numbers.

4.12.35
Miss Burwell resigned to go to Burbage Infants School. 16 applications, 4 to be interviewed.

30.12.35
Miss I.Swindin of Doncaster appointed for the new term.

6.7.36
The Managers had visited since the appointment of the new Headmistress. There were several items on which they were not entirely satisfied. She was interviewed and these points were brought to her notice.

School Group 1936

25.10.37
There were reports of the unpunctuality of the Headmistress. On the day of the meeting she did not arrive till 9.05, and this had happened on several occasions. Miss Swindin said she had not been aware of being late.
There were complaints of bad language being used by the children in the playground and outside.
The Managers had interviewed her about her general conduct in the school and her unpunctuality, and recommended her replacement.

7.3.38
Miss Swindin had not resigned, so she was given notice effective on the last day of 1938.

18.3.38
Miss Rose A.Adamson from Oxted, Surrey was appointed.

19.6.39
Frequent coughs and colds were suffered by the Fuller family, and the Medical Officer's attention was drawn to it to see if there were some infection.

15.4.40
'This is a good school', said HMI Mr.R.D.S.Davidson. It was an excellent report, and Miss Adamson was congratulated.
On roll - 14.

21.1.43
Miss Adamson resigned to go to Peckleton Council School. There were 2 applicants, and Mrs.Symonds of South Croxton, a Certificated Teacher, was appointed.

30.10.44
School efficiency - it was recorded that an appreciation of her good work would be conveyed to Mrs.Symonds. A very happy atmosphere prevailed throughout the school, and excellent results were being attained.

Mrs.Symonds with the school 1945.

1.7.46
A letter of congratulation was sent to Mrs.Symonds on highly satisfactory results achieved in the qualifying exams for Secondary School, as well as the improved condition of the playgrounds and school gardens.

1.7.47
A development plan was produced, in which South Croxton School was to close and the children sent to Gaddesby.
On 30.6.47 and 15.12.47 Mrs Symonds was congratulated on the hard work shown by the children.

21.4.49
The clerk was asked to write to the Council to enquire whether toilet rolls could be provided for use by the children.

15.5.49
- they could, and 6 had been sent to the school.

16.5.49
Water was obtained from a nearby house - could the school have its own water supply?

26.9.49
- no, not before Summer 1950.

12.6.50
Letter of congratulations sent to Mrs.Symonds on the examination results.
(The examination was for the QESS – the Queen Elizabeth School Scholarship, and under Mrs.Symonds, 1 or 2 passed each year.)

In the Spring of 1955 the earth toilet closets were replaced by Elsan closets, though the managers protested that water closets were preferable.

19.3.56
The managers were J.E.Sherrif as the County Council representative, Rev.F.Clarke, Messrs Barsby and Kirk, and Lady Earle, who never attended.

29.11.56
HMI Mr.Halifax visited for a short time, and on 21.1.57.

25.5.56
Mrs.Symonds was taken ill, and replaced by Mrs.E.Glover of Syston; she found the atmosphere a very happy one. The children worked well, and standards were equivalent to those in other schools, particularly the younger ones. She also remarked that she found it very lonely.

14.7.58
Mrs Draycott, school cook since 1946, returned after two operations, resulting in one eye being removed.

24.2.60
The sudden death of Mrs.Symonds before the Christmas holidays was reported.
There was one applicant for the post, Miss Dover.

13.7.60
Miss Dover reported that some of the older boys were being very troublesome.

23.11. 60
Parent-teacher liaison and the managers felt that the boy whose behaviour was troublesome due to his indiscipline should be transferred to Queniborough who had a male in charge, and he would be with boys of his own age. The Senior Educational Psychologist had been to see another boy who was rather troublesome and backward. Since the meeting between parent, managers and teacher the work of one of the boys had improved considerably.

19.12.62
It was reported that the school cook, Mrs.Draycott, had died and her husband appointed instead.

Miss Dover with the school 1962

Miss Dover placed an order for the erection of a screen across the entrance to the boys' toilets.

Mrs.Winnick was appointed Head from September 1961.

25.6.61
Rev. Ian Phelps reported that he had been most impressed with the atmosphere in the school since Mrs. Winnick had been appointed.

28.11.63
16 on roll, average age seven and a half.
French introduced on the curriculum.
Mrs.Douet, Principal Lecturer in Primary Education at the Leicester Teacher Training College at Scraptoft visited with a view to placing students at the school on Teaching Practice.
It was arranged for Mrs.Griffiths, former Head of Barsby school, to visit each week for two hours to give music lessons.
Mrs.Darnford, kitchen assistant since 1955, was leaving.

The Assistant Director was asked if the house next to the school could be purchased(5).

Two students from Scraptoft came on Teaching Practice from November 11th. To 17th on a preliminary visit, and would come In February for three weeks. Rev.Phelps would accommodate them.

Jan 65
A telephone was installed in the school and a tape recorder was delivered.

7.1.65
The Director of Education, Mr.Fairbairn, attended to warn of the closure of South Croxton and Barsby Schools, and the transfer of the children to Gaddesby. It was policy to close all one-teacher schools. Any local organisation, e.g.the Village Hall Committee, would be given priority to purchase.

26,11,65
The modernisation of the school continues with the supply of two Towelmasters.
The Buildings and Sites Committee of the Education Department of the County Council told the Board that the District Valuer had placed a value of £8,500 on the school site and building. A referendum was taken of the villagers; 103 voted for purchase, 9 for building a new village hall on the site of the present one.

March 1966
Miss Slipton and Miss Thomas had been on teaching practice from the Leicester Training College from January 17th. To February 11th.

10.10.66
Mr.Cooper took an 8mm. film of the children.

15.9.66
The official notice concerning the closure of the school was pinned to the front door.

18.2.67
'From January 16th. Till February 10th. We had two mature students from Leicester Training College, Mr.Cork and Mr.Ramsey. The children benefited a great deal from this, exploring the theme of Robin Hood, helping to make a real bow and arrow, digging up fossils on North Manor Farm, and playing real football.'

Jim Cork and David Ramsey on teaching Practice from the City of Leicester Training College

14.3.67
Mrs.Griffiths left and Miss Kendall started music.

Because numbers would rise to 23, another teacher would be required. This was to be Mrs.Hare who had just moved into the village, and would teach part-time in the mornings only, during the Summer Term.

The County Architect had inspected the premises and had arranged for a new soakaway to be constructed so that rainwater could be diverted from the cesspit, which would have to be emptied less frequently.

On June 7th.1967 an article appeared in the Leicester Mercury and the Melton Times about the last open day at the school. The children had sung songs, and performed a play in French for the parents, and later children, dressed as they had done in a photo taken about 1905, with the girls in their smocks, had given a PE display followed by a modern lesson in ordinary dress.

The children would not return after Christmas, but a bus would collect them from opposite the Golden Fleece to take them to Gaddesby School. The Christmas term ended with a play and carols, but before that, £4.5s.0d. was spent on hiring a coach to take the school to a pantomime, and after 3s.11d. was spent on sweets, the School Account was empty, and closed.

The old school, now the Village Hall.

Appendix

Numbers on roll.

1907	51
1917	31 (5 more soon)
1919	29
1935	15
1940	40
1952	10
1953	9
1954	7
1955	11
1963	19
1963	16 - average age 7.5yrs.
1964	20
1965	22
1967	23

Notes

(1) A Supplementary Teacher was untrained. They could be recognised only in a particular school, and this recognition could be withdrawn at any time. Often they taught only the younger ones, the under 8s. The Head Teacher taught the rest.

(2) An Uncertificated Teacher was one who would get a qualification as soon as possible. This was a provisional measurement at the time, and occurred often in rural schools.

(3) Monitors were senior children who had been taught by rote by the teacher, and them went on to teach the younger children. In this way, it was claimed, 100 children could be taught by one teacher. “If it is not cheap it is efficient; if it is not efficient it is cheap.” …debate on the 1880 Education Act.

(4) A Pupil Teacher was someone who had received a Secondary education up to the age of 16. and who learnt to teach by 'standing at Nelly's elbow'. This was a saying taken from the mills of Lancashire where new workers were told to stand by someone, see how they did it, and then went and did it themselves. The Pupil Teachers went regularly to Pupil Teacher Centres, and eventually became qualified. Today, we seem to have gone back to this system of training teachers for many, with school based training after a degree, whereas from the early 60s many got B.Ed.degrees over three or four years, and it was called 'Teacher Education', a significant change in concept.

(5) The house, now called 'The Old School House', was never owned by the Education Authority, nor the school, although at least one Headmistress, Mrs.Symonds, lived there with her family. It is not unreasonable to suppose that other teachers had lived there before. The answer from County Hall is not recorded, although with the imminent closure of the school it was unlikely to have been favourable.

Some idea about the funding of the school can be gained from some remaining notes of the grants allotted, which depended on the report of the Inspectors. Grants were made by the Government through the Board of Education in the money of the day.
A note on money for those whose memory does not go back to pre-1972:
Prior to decimalisation in 1972 money was calculated in pounds, shillings and pence.
There were 20 shillings in the pound, and 12 pence in a shilling.
Coins were a farthing (¼ of a penny), a halfpenny (pronounced hay-penny) a threepenny bit (pronounced thrip'ny - a joey), sixpence (a tanner), a shilling (a bob), two shillings (two bob), half a crown or two[shillings] and sixpence, a ten shilling note (ten bob) in orange/red, a pound note (a quid) in blue. A five pound note was a rarity, and was large and white.

The sum of a guinea (one pound and one shilling) was still used, mostly in business, but the coin representing it had been discontinued long before.
Writing money: £, or the 'L' for the Latin 'Libra' was used for pounds and, as now, came before the number. 's' for shillings, and 'd' for pence, which stood for the Latin 'denaruis', came after the number.
The gaps or divisions between pounds and shillings, and shillings and pence were noted by a '.' or '/'.
If there were no pence the convention was to use '.' or '0'.
The conventions of using '/' for the divisions, using '0' for no pence is used below, as was the custom at the time.

Originals of the following are in the possession of Mrs.Maude Nicol.

17th.May 1886

The Report of Her Majesty's Inspector has been received, and payment of grant allowed, according to the following schedule:

Average attendance: Boys 23.3
Girls 24.9
Total 48.3

Fixed grant: 4/6d.
Merit (1/-, 2/-, 3/-) 2/0
Singing 6d.
<u>Elementary subjects:</u>
Percentage of passes 7/10d.
<u>Class subjects:</u>
English, (1/- or 2/- each) 1/0d
Grant on total Average Attendance: 15/10d.
Grant for needlework 25/0.

Present for examination 37.
Absent without excuse 0.
Passed in Reading 37
Writing 36
Arithmetic 31
Total 104

Schedule of grants for 14 months:
On average attendance £44/6/8d.
Plus £31/9/2d.

Grant under Article 11: £11/13/5d.
Gross total of claim: £57/9/2d.

Summary of Inspector's Report on the school:
"The school has made a good beginning, especially in the Elementary Subjects".

25th.April 1887

The Report of Her Majesty's Inspector has been examined, and a payment of grant allowed, according to the following schedule:

Average attendance: Boys 19.1
Girls 30.6
Total 50

Fixed Grant 4/6d.
Merit 1/-, 2/-, 3/- 2/0d.
Singing 6d.
Elementary Subjects:
Percentage of passes 8/0d.
Class subjects:
English 1/- or 2/0 2/0` d.
Geography 2/-

Grant on total average attendance 19/0d.

£11.13.6d.

Present for examination 35
Absent without excuse 0
Passes in reading 35
Writing 34
Arithmetic 31
Total 104

Schedule of grants for 14 months £44/6/8d.
Plus £1/9/2d.

Grant under Article 11

(As a consequence, the teacher's salary would have decreased - another consequence of 'payment by results' which started in 1862, and continued for most of the rest of the century. Now we have SATs and league tables to increase accountability.

The school with Mrs.Winnett 1963

16 The Village Hall

During the 1914-1918 War a Territorial Army Drill Hut made of wood was built on the site of 12/14 School Lane. When it was no longer needed for its original purpose it became the Village Hall. No documents are available for this period. In the 1960s it had become dilapidated. It was rat infested underneath. The then Director of Education visited the school on the 7th.January 1965 to answer questions about its closure. He assured the village that any village organisation, for example, the Village Hall Committee, would have first refusal when it came to selling the school building. The County Valuer had put a price of £8,500 on the property. Later in the same year it was decided by a vote that the village should purchase the property, and that the money needed for its purchase should be raised. Plans were drawn up by the Re-Building Committee for the conversion of the building to its changed use

The village set about finding the money needed for the former school. Fundraising in the village started in January 1964. The account was closed in November 1972. The sale of the old site raised £1,100. Fundraising events included dances, whist drives, football sweeps, raffles, sales of cakes, a skittles week, and, memorably, a Village Fete which was opened by a television personality of the time, 'Farmer' Ted Moult.

<u>*SOUTH CROXTON FETE MAY 30, 1964.*</u>

On Saturday, May 30, 1964, a fete took place in South Croxton in aid of the village hall building fund. The fete was held in the grounds of Zion House, on Main Street, and was opened by the television personality, Ted Moult. The fete commenced at 2.45 p.m., and it was opened by Mr. Moult at 3 p.m.

The official programme cost 1/-, or 5p in today's money, and the programme admitted to the fete. The official programme of events was as follows –

2.45 p.m. PARADE OF MELTON MOWBRAY TOY SOLDIERS' BAND THROUGH THE VILLAGE.
3 p.m. FETE OFFICIALLY OPENED BY MR. TED MOULT.
4 p.m. TEAS AND REFRESHMENTS SERVED IN THE MARQUEE, HOT SNACKS AT BOY SCOUTS' BUFFET.
4.15 p.m. DISPLAY BY TOY SOLDIES
5.30 p.m. LUCKY PROGRAMME NUMBER, GRAND PRIZE DRAW.
8.00 p.m. DANCING TO THE RANGERS.

During the afternoon, there was a clay pigeon shoot organised by Mr.W.Smith, with stilton cheese as prizes. Mr.Jim Elliott of the Golden Fleece organised a tug of war for a barrel of beer, and Bowley's staff opposed the Crawford staff in this contest.

Other entertainments and stalls were individual skittling for live pig, the pig given by Mr. N. Whittle ; team skittling for supper, the supper given by Mr. S.Crawford; take home tomorrow's dinner - win a cockerel by simply cutting the string; how good are you at Hoop - la? knock off the man's top hat; bottle stall; win at bingo; tennis balls in the bucket; smash those pots; have a throw at table skittles; try the devil among the tailors; take home your portrait by a local artist; tin stall; pitching horse shoes; guess the weight of cake and number of sweets in jar; guess the doll's name; pony ride ; lucky dip; rifle range.

A whist drive in the village hall had taken place as part of the same programme of events on Monday, May 25, 1964, commencing at 8 p.m.

The village hall committee at the time of the 1964 fete was as follows -

President Mr.N Catlow; Chairman Mr R.Moore ; Secretary MrT.Proctor ; Treasurer - Mrs. F. Bowley; Committee Members – Mrs. F.Townsley, Messrs M.Baxter, F.Bowley, D.Bradbury, K.Catlow, S.Coultate, S.Crawford, J.Elliott, J.Little and J.Roberts.

In the fete programme, the President, Mr. Norman Catlow, wrote:

" I would like to extend a warm welcome to all who come to our garden fete this afternoon, and we are indeed fortunate in having such an outstanding personality as Mr Ted Moult, of T.V. fame, who needs no introduction from me, to open it. And we are grateful to him for sparing the time to come along and assist our efforts, which I am sure his presence will do.

As you probably know, the entire proceeds are going towards a new Village Hall, which we are hoping to start on as soon as sufficient funds are available. It will be erected on the site of the old one, which has done duty for well over 40 years; it was originally an old 1914-1918 Army Hut, so has done good service in more ways than one, but after such long use it is not surprising that it has almost reached a state beyond repair.

It has been a great asset to the village for such functions as Dances, Whist Drives, the Drama Group, and Women's Institute Meetings, to name only a few, all of which raise money at different times for charities, and with the growth of the population of the village, which includes many more young people, these functions are likely to increase rather than diminish. We feel they deserve a more modern and up-to-date hall in which to hold their various social activities, and we are hoping today to raise a good sum towards that purpose.

I therefore look forward to your support in this worthy object and hope you will find plenty to interest you in the many side shows that are listed in the programme, and feel sure that an afternoon spent in the lovely countryside of this delightful part of Leicestershire will be in itself worthwhile."

NORMAN S. CATLOW
President of the South Croxton Village Hall Fund.

It is evident from this that it was proposed to build a new Village Hall on the site of the old, but this was obviously overtaken by other decisions. A Leicester Mercury article of 14th.January 1972 said that planning permission to rebuild on the old site was not obtained because of the lack of parking space, and that grants were expected from the Ministry of Education and Science, and the Barrow Rural Council. In the event, the old school cost £8,452.

Through these events, private donations, with interest added, the sum had grown to £2,847, according to the accounts of the committee. However, it is at odds with the Leicester Advertiser piece on July 16th.1976, which says that the village collected £8,500. In all probability the total cost of the building was £8,500, of which £6,500 was procured through grants. On 20th.June 1972, Leicestershire County Council sold the former school and its playground to the trustees - Stanley Crawford of South Manor Farm, Malcolm Arthur Green of 47, Mansion Court Gardens, Thorne near Doncaster, Norman Crawford of South Manor Farm, and William John Little of Hill Top Farm. The Conveyance and Trust Deed said that the Village Hall was to be used '...for meetings, lectures and classes and for other forms of recreation and leisure-time occupation with the object of improving the conditions of life for the said inhabitants.' The organisations noted in the Deed were the Parish Meeting, the Committee of the Women's Institute, The Parochial Church Council, the Committee of the Youth Club, Young Marrieds Organisation (which no longer existed), the Ancient Order of Foresters, Ladies Keep Fit Class and the Ladies Guild.

A Re-Building Committee was set up to oversee the change of the building to suit its new purpose. At a Parish Meeting held in the Church on 20th.June 1972 five parishioners agreed to form the basis of a new Management Committee to take over the responsibility of running the Village Hall once it was completed. Until then the Re-Building Committee was to continue, was to arrange the opening ceremony, and would then be disbanded.

The old Village Hall needed dismantling. The easiest way to do this was to set it alight. It was burnt down in late1972, and Freda Elliott, seeing it, went to get a camera, and took a number of shots of the burning building. There are no photographs of the building as it was originally.

The first meeting of the new Village Hall Committee took place on 29th.June 1972 in 'The Hall', which presumably was the old Village Hall. Mr.W.McOwen was in the chair, Mr.F.Robinson was the secretary, and other members were Mrs.E.McOwen, Mrs.F.Simmonds, and Mrs.M.Aldis. They discussed representative members of local organisations, the official opening ceremony, insurances, functions with bar facilities, the winter programme and fund raising activities.

The next meeting was held at Barley Leys in School Lane, the house of the secretary, on September 15th.1972, so presumably the Hall was not available and had probably been burnt down by that date. The Winter programme was discussed, among which was an illustrated talk by Terry Pearce, the leader of the Archaeological Team which had been excavating the moated site.

The first meeting in the new Village Hall took place on 6th.October 1972. At it a vote of thanks was given to the village children and other helpers who had cleaned up the Village Hall prior to the start of classes in September. The secretary had attended a site meeting with the builder, the architect and the Re-Building Committee, and reported that all the outstanding work and all faults would be rectified by 21st.October 1972.

By its meeting on 3rd.November 1972 no date had been fixed for the official opening. It was reported that Terry Pearce had given a talk of the South Croxton dig on 13th.October, that 70 people had attended, and that Mr.Pearce had donated his fee to the Village Hall. Keep Fit and Art classes were continuing, and reports were received of arrangements for a New Years Eve Function, a Rural Studio presented by the Leicestershire Rural Community Council, the Evergreen Group visit to a production of ‘Oliver’ at Wreake College, W.I. ’As New’ sale, a Grand Christmas Draw, a Fur and Feather Whist Drive, and a Children’s New Year Party.

By 10th.January, still no date had been fixed for the official opening, and arrangements were made to hire the hall as a polling station for Local Elections.

The Hall was finally officially opened on 30th.May 1973. There remains just a minute to record this event, and no other evidence such as photographs or official announcement has yet been discovered. However, in a piece in the Leicester Advertiser about the Arts Festival and the village published on July 16th.1976, it notes that it was the Lord Lieutenant of Leicestershire, Colonel Andrew Martin, who opened the hall, and in his remarks said, ”This Village Hall is a story of great and long endeavour.” Another of July 1973 says that 90 people attended the opening, and that Col. Martin praised the village, which contained just over 200 people, for raising such a sum of money.

Early on in the minutes there is note of a recurring theme, how to encourage more interest in the use of the Village Hall, and therefore its income. Coffee mornings, discos and film shows were discussed.

At the meeting of 6th.June 1973 John Redfern proposed an open air Art Exhibition - the precursor of the South Croxton Arts Festival. In his contribution to the piece about the Festival in this booklet, John Redfern notes that…".. the Village Hall came to rely more and more on the hard earned profit from the event. Over the years it paid for a new extension, the renewal of the roof (with some grant aid), the new storage area, improvements to the electrical heating, and finally the introduction of full gas central heating. At one stage, due to the Festival, the children of the village were able to enjoy recorder and guitar lessons, and have subsidies for several children's parties and fireworks celebrations. At one time we even explored the possibility of employing a Youth Leader." The last Festival took place in 2002, and since then the Village Hall Committee has struggled to keep it going on the proceeds from parties, entertainment and other events. There has even been talk of demolishing it and rebuilding something with the facilities and space appropriate for the 21st.century.

In April 2005 the Parish Council noted that the Village Hall Committee was defunct, took over the running of the hall, and commissioned a report on its state, appropriateness for its function, and value as a building plot.

On Sunday 26th.July 2005 there was a meeting in the Village Hall concerning its future. It was attended by 24 people, representing 18 households, or roughly 20% of the village. It was agreed that a Village Hall was required as a centre for village activities, but that the present building was unsuited for the purpose. It would need a complete refurbishment, or a replacement, either on the present site or elsewhere. A refurbishment cost of £70,000 had been obtained from the survey commissioned by the parish Council.

Six volunteers joined the new committee set up to review short term needs and social events, and determine the future for the Village Hall.

Village Hall entrance

17 South Croxton Arts Festival

Poster advertising the second festival in 1976 designed and produced by John Redfern

At a meeting of the Village Hall Committee on 6th June 1973 John Redfern proposed an Art Exhibition - the precursor of the South Croxton Arts Festival. This took place on 24th and 25th August 1974, in the Village Hall and outside. Between 700 and 800 people visited, and the profit from entrance fees and commission on sales, after expenses had been deducted, was £53.26. The intention was to make it an annual event. At the South Croxton Arts Festival held in 1975, 2000 people attended.

It became a biennial event starting in 1978. It grew in numbers attending and in reputation, and eventually took over the whole village. By 1988 the number of visitors had reached 3,000 - an easy number to calculate as there were no concessions that year. In 1990 there was no festival as the caterer had to withdraw at the last moment. As John Redfern was arranging everything on his own, he decided that it could not run. It was later suggested by Phil Snelders that a committee be selected to aid him. This was set up under the chair of Brian Piper. As result the festival expanded. and took over the whole village. There were prestigious performances at the church, notably by 'Not Pavarotti', four professional singers who offered a medley of light classical pieces, a jazz band in the Golden Fleece, another at no.23 Main St. where teas were served, dancing and musical performances in the playground of the former school and in the marquee, a sculpture trail through the village for children, a mock 'Scrufts' where dogs were jokingly judged, open gardens, and many other events. Sadly, in 2002, because of very poor weather, the attendance was low, the event just covered its costs, John Redfern had retired from the committee in 2000 taking his expertise in art with him, and the chair, Brian Piper, who had been at the helm since 1991, the beginning of the organisation of the 1992 Festival, retired in 2002. There being no one else found to head the organising committee, the event ceased.

John Redfern has contributed the following:

"The idea of an Arts Festival was first proposed as a way of making more use of the Village Hall; and the exhibitions were put together by my family and artist friends. At the time there were several talented individuals living in or near the village. For example, the dolls made by Maud Nicol were very popular for many years, as were the welded butterflies made by Bill and Peter Cockburn, who for several years ran a welding business near the Church. Marion Aldis, who ran a very popular and successful Pottery from Zion House in the village, also made a significant contribution to the early years of the festival. Two self-taught painters from Barsby, Mary Preston and Rosemary Holt, also made a valuable contribution.

The success of the first festival surprised and enthused us, and each year we became more and more ambitious, and our audience grew and grew, so that at the tenth Festival in 1988 we registered an attendance of over 3,000.

Most of the artists whose work we displayed were professional.

But from time to time we found incredibly talented self-taught artists. We also displayed work by artists and illustrators whose work was known nationally and internationally - but not in their own Leicestershire. Some of the most exciting, challenging and controversial art was being produced in our own Art Colleges, and I enjoyed seeing their work and inviting the most original of them to exhibit at our Festival. Some of the best work was being done by sculptors, and we were one of the first organisation to realise that, put into our lovely indoor and outdoor settings, how stimulating this would be for our visitors.

Meanwhile the Village Hall came to rely more and more on the hard earned profit from the event. Over the years it paid for a new extension, the renewal of the roof (with some grant aid), the new storage area, improvements to the electrical heating, and finally the introduction of full gas central heating. At one stage, due to the Festival, the children of the village were able to enjoy recorder and guitar lessons, and have subsidies for several children's parties and fireworks celebrations. At one time we even explored the possibility of employing a Youth Leader.

I am sorry the Festival has not been able to continue but have always realised that it is an enormous task for a volunteer committee to organise. However, I still get enormous pleasure from seeing exhibitions, booklets and reproductions of the work of artists we have featured at South Croxton over the years. This year for instance, Unesco reproduced the work of Kate Follows for their cards and commissioned her to design their Christmas decorations, and Rachel Higgins was commissioned to produce sculptural work for the Victoria and Albert Museum.

In 1998 we featured the work of a young student from Wreake Valley College. This year (2005) that young student, Glen Boulter, graduates from the Royal College of Art."

John Redfern

Scaf Committee 1996

Back Row:
Brian Piper, John Redfern, Phil Snelders, Karen McNeelance, Bruce Attenborough

Front Row:
Annette Piper, Nicky Ainscough, Heidi Seary

18 The Golden Jubilee Obelisk

In the middle of the village half way up the hill, is a mini obelisk celebrating the Queen's Golden Jubilee. Closer examination of the commemorative brass plaques show it was unveiled by the village children on the 12th. July 2005, three years later. For a more detailed explanation of the intervening years, go to the account lodged in the Village Archive. The press release announcing the unveiling simply attributed the delay to discussion about where to site it.

The original idea was for a village sign, modelled on those commonly found throughout East Anglia, appeared in an issue of the South Croxton Clarion some time earlier (issue 24, July 1995) and was taken up by the South Croxton Arts Festival Committee as a memorial to the millennium but they failed to get sufficient funding. They revived the idea for the Queen's Golden Jubilee in 2002 and this time sufficient funding was obtained, mainly from the lottery 'Awards for All', Leicestershire County Council 'Shire Grants', and the committee's own resources, plus later a supplementary grant from Charnwood Borough Council.

All the village children and young people up to 18 years old were invited to make a ceramic tile to go on the obelisk with their names, showing their view of the village in the year of the Queen's Golden Jubilee. Local artists Lisa Denham from Loughborough and Nita Rao from Mountsorrel were commissioned to work with the children in the design and execution of the tiles. The original plan was to make it a summer holiday project to be exhibited at the 2002 Arts Festival over the August Bank Holiday. However, the wheels of committee cycles moved too slowly and the Lottery money only became available on the eve of the bank holiday, so the youngsters and the artists did their work over the October half-term break and subsequent weekends. From the outset, parents and children were very enthusiastic and supportive, and 34 of them participated in big and small ways out of a possible 43.

Beginning with much discussion and designs on paper, ideas took shape and were transferred to clay images and the colours subsequently added. The brief to the artists was to work with the concept of an obelisk which emerged as a three sided figure some two metres high. The design evolved more as a cooperative venture, and being a children's eye view of the village, as well as recording its farming life, the playing field and brook figured quite prominently with the brook revealing some very exotic fish! Village landmarks were also recorded, such as the village hall and the Golden Fleece. The artists worked to create a coherent whole from the efforts of youngsters from 18 months to 18 years, with colours which would fit in with surrounding grass and meadows.

Over succeeding months there were several displays of the work at the various stages from original firing to final glazing. The finished tiled were displayed in September 2003 in the village hall. 54 villagers visited and gave their enthusiastic endorsement. The artists then went away to build the concrete core onto which the tiles would be stuck and the bronze cladding and cap.

After a long period of debate and negotiations with the Parish

Council and various local government departments, agreement was reached on where to put it. To huge sighs of relief, it was finally lowered into place on the 8th. of June 2005 and unveiled the following weekend followed by a party for the youngsters in the village hall, paid for by the Parish Council. More than one parent was overheard telling their offspring that they would be able to come back in years to come and show their children and grandchildren how they celebrated the Golden Jubilee of Queen Elizabeth II. I suppose monuments do have that potential to be a focus for memories.

Brian Piper (for South Croxton Arts Festival Committee)

Children who participated

Katie (7) and Ben (5) Aldridge
Sam (10) and Annie (7) Brunskill
Aisha (15) and Imran (12) Farooqui
Harry (11) and Jack (9) Forfar
Sara (14), Ted (13) and Patrick (9) Harris
Imogen (3) and Scarlet (18 months) Langford
Adam (7) and Bethan (3) Lewis
Jane (5) and Kate (3) Loughran
Ellen (6) and Gabrielle (4) McNeelance
Amy (9) and Hollie (4) Marriott
Rebecca (6) and Oliver (3) Moore
Sam (11) and Mat (9) Spokes
Elizabeth Charles (6)
Charlie Campbell (3)
Emma Fox (11)
Rochelle Harris (12)
Martin Jackson (15)
Joshua (4) and Charlotte (18 months) Johnson

Unveiling of QEII Jubilee Obelisk

19 The Vintage Tractor and Engine Working Weekend

(Every year in August there is a 'Working Weekend' in fields near the village. These fields are normally on Crawford's fields, but sometimes they are on Frank Black's fields.)

The annual Vintage and Tractor and Engine Working Weekend was born in 1989, following an invitation by Mr.Norman Crawford, who farmed at South Manor Farm South Croxton, to members of the Rutland Vintage Tractor Club, to bring their machines and have them working in one of his fields.

Since that time, many thousands of visitors from all corners of the British Isles have come to this little corner of Leicestershire from the young, who have been fascinated by the old machinery, and seeing a history of bygone days revealed to them, to those who have turned back the clock to their younger days, with pleasant memories of yesteryear, seeing horses ploughing the fields, the smell of steam, the modern machinery working in nearby fields, evoking memories of these machines, and the way of life they provided. **Ann Crawford**

Village view uphill

20 The Women's Institute

http://www.womens-institute.co.uk/
http://www.womens-institute.co.uk/leicestershire

The National Federation of Women's Institutes is the largest national organisation for women in the UK with 220,000 members in England, Wales and the Islands. The ideals of the Women's Institute of truth, justice, tolerance and fellowship are as strong and important now in the 21st century as they were at the birth of the WI in 1915. The WI exists to educate women to enable them to provide an effective role in the community, to expand their horizons and to develop and pass on important skills.

The Leicestershire and Rutland Federation has Institutes throughout both counties, including two institutes within the city and at least one institute in all our market towns, we have the rural areas well covered. Like other federations our members and institutes come in all shapes, sizes and ages. Art and Crafts, Public Affairs, Sport and Leisure, Music, Home Economics, Food, Social Events, in fact any interest that members have in any aspect, we do our very best to accommodate and encourage them.

In the South Croxton Institute the emphasis is on providing a wide range of interesting speakers and activities, friendship, and last but by no means least, wonderful refreshments at every meeting!

Angela Stephens
President

Tel: (01664) 840152   E-mail: amwstephens@aol.com

The South Croxton Women's Institute was started in May 1941 by Mrs.Clark, the wife of the then Rector, who was its President from then until 1957.

For the first few years many of the Institute's activities were in response to the shortages experienced during the Second World War. There were 'Make-Do-And-Mend' classes, and talks of 'Clothes Economy', and 'Rag Bag Toy Making'. Freda Elliott, who was a Founder Member, recalls making slippers from old felt hats. There was a distribution of vegetable seeds, and members collected medicinal herbs and rose hips. Difficulties with transport are frequently mentioned in the minutes, and some ladies cycled to a group meeting at Tilton.

After the war the W.I. was able to arrange an annual outing to the seaside for the children of the village. For many years they also ran a children's Christmas party, and sometimes a visit to the pantomime too. Adults were not forgotten – in the early 1960s there was a Christmas dance, and pensioners received a Christmas parcel, or, later, W.I. calendars.

At that time there were about thirty five members, although the village was much smaller than it is today; now there are only fifteen of us, and we would be delighted to welcome new members.

Most of our meetings have been held in the Village Hall - the old hall or the present one - but some have been at the school (before the building became the Village Hall), the Rectory, and the Golden Fleece, and others at members' houses. In the early days fires had to be lit beforehand to warm the hall, and sometimes the lights would go out during the meeting if we had not fed the meter with enough coins.

Speakers at our monthly meetings have told us about a wide variety of subjects, ranging from cookery and gardening to history and travel. In January we have often invited someone in the village to tell us about their job, and these have proved to be some of the most interesting meetings. In the Summer months we have been on guided walks and visits to places of interest.

In May we have always held our Birthday Party; at one time this was at the Village Hall, but now we usually visit a pub or restaurant. We also have a meal out after Christmas, and a theatre visit has often been arranged.

Our Institute is one of eight in the Robin-on-Tiptoe Group, and members from each village attend a spring meeting with a speaker, and an autumn social gathering. Since 1990 the group has held a carol service in one of the churches, and this is always an enjoyable occasion.

The minutes of W.I. meetings over the years record many village events, and although they sometimes mention minor disagreements, the main impression is of co-operation among women living here, enjoyment of very varied activities, and friendship.

Sue Groocock
Secretary
Tel: (01664) 840418.

Village view uphilll

21 The Wednesday Club

About ten years ago it was noted by the Parish Council that there was no amenity in the village for the elderly group of residents. and I was asked to arrange something. I arranged tea and cake in the Village Hall, followed by a speaker. Each person paid 50p.each meeting, and for a few years it was quite popular. However, the Village Hall was cold in winter, and the group tried to pay towards the cost of heating each year, but this left very little from the subscriptions to give a donation to charity on behalf of the speakers. These were very good, and many of them were village residents.

The numbers were limited; twelve was a very good turnout, but eight was the usual number attending. Outings were very popular, and visits were paid to Chatsworth House, Burghley House at Stamford, the Mount St. Bernard Monastery at Whitwick and many more.

About five years ago, I thought that the organisation was getting too onerous, so I called a meeting my house at which I announced my decision. All were concerned, and it was decided that the group should go out to lunch once a month to keep the Wednesday Club alive. This proved popular, and the Club now exists as a Luncheon Club, meeting every other month, each member in turn choosing and booking the venue.

The club is open to anyone from the village, and lifts can be arranged.

Previous meetings:

About a dozen members meet every other month, and have been for lunch, among other places, to:

South Croxton, the Golden Fleece;

Houghton, Rose & Crown;
Keyham, Dog & Gun;
Knossington, Fox & Hounds;
Hamilton, the Finch's Arms;
Medborne, Neville Arms;
Hoby, Blue Bell Inn;
Cold Overton, Gates Nursery;
Hungarton, Black Boy.

Contact: Rita Ross 840478

Vonnie Gardner

22 Memories

(In this section are recorded memories by inhabitants and former inhabitants of the village. The first is in an undated, but signed note left by Mrs.R.J.Freer, who lived at the Thatched Cottage. The date is probably in the late 1930s.)

Mrs.R.J.Freer

South Croxton

When the spire of South Croxton church was struck by lightning in 1936 a landmark known to all who travel to East Leicestershire disappeared. Happily the spire has been restored by the efforts of Rev.Clarke and his parishioners., and once more stands like a beckoning finger at the top of the hill up which the village struggles from the Croxton brook.

South Croxton is a happy example of the unspoilt agricultural village, of a type which is fast disappearing from the English countryside. It has no squire, no 'big house', no industries, nor has it any desire for any of these things. The great majority if its inhabitants still earn their living in and around the village and remain content to be a modestly self-supporting community, sustained more by ties of friendship than by patronage or external organisation.

The village has its roots in antiquity. Formerly called Crochestone, or Crowson-juxta-Baggrave – the name of South Croxton was presumably given to it when Croxton Kerriat became a centre of religious importance in Leicestershire – it is mentioned in Edward the Confessor's survey when it is recorded as having a mill.

Its golden ironstone church is Early English, but has a Norman font dating to about 1120, of a rare architectural style. Although there are no historical relics in the village, it is easy to read the passing of history in the moat behind the church, presumably the site of one of those fortified farmhouses which were so common in the Middle Ages, and in the remains of earthworks at the back of the Main Street, believed to have been thrown up during the Civil War.

As is the case with all truly rural villages, Croxton has lost too many of its cottages in the last half century, and new houses, at a rental within the means of the agricultural worker, are an essential need to the continued existence of the village.

Given piped water supply and better communication with the towns, a more substantial village hall, South Croxton will rest content to remain a stronghold of the true English village life.

(Mrs.) R.J.Freer, Thatched Cottage, South Croxton

Mrs.Catherine Roberts

(Mrs.Roberts was interviewed by Roy King and Chris Stanyard on June 16th.1980 at her home in Main Street.)

Mrs.Catherine Mary Roberts was born in Beeby in 1905, as Catherine Mary Naylor. When she was two years old she moved to South Croxton. Her father went to work as a shepherd at South Manor Farm, and, when Catherine left school ay 13 in 1918, she went to work there in the cheese room. At school in the village she told of the discipline, and how the boys would bow to the teachers, and the girls curtsey.

She remembered School Lane, and a row of cottages where the council houses are now. Between no.7 and no.9 there was a butcher's shop, and on the site of no.5 a scrap yard. In her younger days the Quorn hunt met in the village on the last day of the year.

She proudly tells of knowing Prince Edward, the Prince of Wales (later King Edward VII and Duke of Windsor) 'very well indeed', as he used to attend the hunt at Melton frequently, and she met the present Prince of Wales, Prince Charles.

She spoke about the blacksmiths at the Golden Fleece, and about people in the village fetching their milk from one of the local farms. She remembered her mother (née Ingram) telling her stories of the past in the village. One she told was of the then Rector, Rev.Noble, who was rector for 25 years from 1868 to 1893, who was conducting a wedding service and tears ran down his cheeks because in the Rectory his wife was dying. Another story was about the great oak cut down in the moat for the Church door.

Her husband, who did much work for the village over the years, died in 1979 at the age of 78 years.

When asked how the village had changed from when she was a young girl, she said, "Not for the better – people had to walk in my young days, there was no such things as cars and such like. The carrier took you to Syston or Leicester, or you walked. So people met each other and talked, and everyone knew everybody. Not today – they get into cars and rush in and out of the village, and you don't know them, and they don't know you."

Mrs.Roberts was vague about dates and years, but gave a lot of information about the village, and the families buried in the churchyard.

This piece was taken from typed noted taken by Roy King.

Mrs.Sybil Barsby and Mrs.Freda Elliott

(Sybil was the daughter of Harrison Kirk of North Manor farm, and sister of Bernard Kirk of Maida House farm, and sister-in-law of Alf Barsby.)

In about 1990 Mrs Sybil Barsby and Mrs.Freda Elliott chatted to Janine Atkins about the village, and it was on tape, some of which is difficult to hear. The following is an account of that conversation. It is in the form of a list of points and statements that were made:

Sybil lived in a cottage 2 up and 2 down. They made Stilton cheese in the cheese room at North Manor - everyone made Stilton cheese; the village was renowned for it. They sold it to a private buyer, Mr.Swain.
When ladies wore hats, they wore a scarf of fine cloth tied under the chin and over the hat - that was the fashion.
The first car Sybil rode in was when she was a girl. It was the car of a representative for agricultural machinery, Mr.Johnson. It couldn't get up the hill, so he turned it round and they reversed up it. It was a little brown car.
Mr.Swain, the cheese factor, had a marvellous car.
The only ones with cars were the Rector, the pub, and Peter Waddington, who worked on the Leicester Mail.
When she got married Sybil moved with her husband into 49, Main Street, which had been built as a shop, though it was not while they stayed there. It later became the shop again. This was the only house built in the village, said Freda's mother, between the wars.
Everyone worked hard. Mrs.Screaton left the village at the beginning of the week, went to another village, spent the week washing, and returned at the end of the week. Once she brought back some potato peelings that had been thickly cut and made part of a meal out of them for her family.
In 1926 there was a general strike and there was no coal. They couldn't thresh till much later. Threshing took three days, and the men had to be fed.
In the war Prisoners of War used to help.
Rats were all over the place at threshing time. Men used to go ratting with their terriers.
Locusts were small, sweet beans which were added to the sheep feed, and the children loved them.

Everything was pure in those days. There were no insecticides, they were not troubled by pests. The cornfields used to be weeded by hand.

There was no violence, or crime. The was some poaching, and someone used to say, “Morrison doesn’t mind as long as it’s done in the daytime.”

Fields used to be full of meadow flowers, and the cornfields of cornflowers. It was all so beautiful. Mrs.Burnaby at Baggrave used to transplant field flowers to the edges of the brook at Baggrave and it looked lovely. Sybil was named after the first Mrs.Burnaby because she was so kind to her father who started to go blind after catching typhoid fever at 20. Her grandmother was also blind, but the kitchen sink and taps were never so clean as when she cleaned them. Typhoid fever was caught from the water - not South Croxton water which was pure, but from Leicester water. Often people who had contracted typhoid fever when young went blind in their 50s.

There was a drought in 1921, and holes were dug at the top of the hill, and the water used to fill the troughs for the cattle. It was clear, beautiful water. Leicester water had chemicals in it.

When they wanted the butter to gather when it was hot they went to the Rector for water from his pump. They had a private buyer for their butter. They made 9lb. a week in the summer, and 40lb. a week in winter.

Apart from the farms there were stocking machines in the village.

The tailor, Mr.Tunnicliffe, lived in Sunny Dene, now called The Old School House.

There was a grocery shop in the farthest cottage of the remaining two in School Lane at the far end of the Westhorpe jitty.

The Moat was an attraction to the children. They loved it. There used to be a plank bridge over it to get to the middle. That was where the great oak grew that was felled for the church door.

Alf Barsby, Sybil’s brother-in-law, was a mine of information about the past of the village.

On fairs and such occasions there was always a skittling match for a pig – usually a small one.

There was a feast on Whit Monday with roundabouts provided by Whites on the paddock behind the pub. There was a march up the hill to the church with the Syston Town Band and banners. Sybil's father was the Chief Ranger of the Ancient Order of Foresters. There was a meal at the Village Hall at which there were great joints of pork and beef.

There were seven cottages downhill from the present cottages, in one of which was a reading room. There were three more at Wheelwrights End in School Lane.

Freda Elliott was born in the cottage opposite the old shop at 49 Main Street.

Sybil Barsby's grandmother, whose maiden name was Morrison, and was born near Balmoral in Scotland, came to the village in 1851 and immediately became a parlourmaid at the Rectory to Rev.Wilkinson.

The village was a poor one, but people ate well in general. On North Manor they bred pigs and horses. It had 147 acres of arable land..

When they went to school there were some good and some indifferent teachers. There were what were called 'object lessons', when you learnt that C-A-T spelled 'cat'. Miss Burrell was a very good teacher. She lived in Syston. Children went to school till 14; the hours were 9-12a.m. and 1.30-4p.m.

Both Sybil and, a generation later, Freda, remembered sledging down the hill at the back of the Rectory. In the war women went to the Rectory for sewing classes.

The pump in the Rectory was outside, and later they had water from taps inside.

The chestnut tree was planted in the Rectory in 1921.

There were hunts that started from the village, to which the Prince of Wales came, and the Queen Mother attended. The Duke of Gloucester and the Duke of Kent fell into the brook on one occasion. Sometimes the hunt would meet on the pub paddock, or on the space now occupied by the council houses.

The rear room of the North Manor Farm was built of the same stone as the Church.

The White House was built for his sister by Rev.Wilkinson. It was of red brick then. Catlow bought it, then the Waldrons then the Maughams.
The Methodist chapel was built on a bank at the far end of the pub car park. It had 9 steps up to it. It was demolished because it was in a dangerous state and likely to fall down. The builder who knocked it down said it would never have fallen down because it was buttressed - they knew what they were doing when they built it.

Mrs.Sybil Barsby and Mrs. Freda Elliott

Freda Elliott remembers the school

Freda Elliott (nee Draycott) attended the school between 1927 and 1933, between the ages of 5 and 11. Miss Rose Black (aunt of Frank Black) taught the younger ones, and Miss Harrison the older ones. She remembered Miss Burrell and Miss Coggon who were later. Miss Burrell was very keen on cleanliness, and had a daily inspection of neck, hands, knees and handkerchiefs. Freda kept her handkerchief for show up her sleeve, and the one for use elsewhere.

There was a wooden partition down the middle of the school room, with a stove on each side of the room. The Juniors were taught on one side and the Seniors on the other. The boys sat separately from the girls.

The playground was also divided down the middle, with the toilets on each side of the building. The boys' was where the kitchens are now. There was a small toilet for the girls, a larger one for the boys, and an even larger one for the teachers.

The teaching and learning was of an elementary kind, with an emphasis on rote learning. It was unheard of that anyone questioned - other than when asked - or refused to do something.

For minor infringements there was a slap with a ruler, for serious ones the cane. There was more to come at home if parents found out, because the punishment brought shame to the family, and there was a great sense of being respectable, of wondering what the neighbours would think. There were no outings. That was the province of the Sunday School, and of the Conservative Association, which arranged trips to Hunstanton or to Skegness.

For many, school was a place to escape from, and eventually to leave.

Freda Elliott

Conversation – Freda Elliott, Fred Draycott, Robert Spokes and Maud Nicol

Freda Elliott, Maude Nicol, Robert Spokes and Fred Draycott at 85 Main Street

(A recording was made in the Autumn of 2004 of a conversation about the village between Freda Elliott, Fred Draycott her brother, Robert Spokes who farmed at The Grange, all of whom were born in the village and went to school here, and Maud Nicol of The Old School House who arrived in the village in 1956. Sadly, Robert died soon afterwards. The conversation is recorded as a list of points made.)

Freda remembered when there was a blacksmith's shop, separated from the pub by and archway in which horses could stand, and barrels of beer were taken through to the rear. Over the archway and blacksmith's shop was a bedroom. In the late 1950s the blacksmith's shop was incorporated into the pub, a door and steps replaced the archway, and a new staircase was built in the living quarters. The building was only single storey at the far end, and this was raised to make two further rooms. In the 1960s a flat roof extension was built at the rear making another room, and the cellar and bar were extended as well as the front, which needed two supporting pillars.
Lucy Muggleton had the cottage nearest to Kings Lane, which is now part of the bar of the Golden Fleece..
There was a trap door through which was the access to the upper rooms but when the Elliotts found rugby players pushing one another through it they had to put a bolt on it.
There was a cesspit in the yard behind the pub, and there was a terrible smell from it, especially on Friday and Saturday nights. It was a pity that the drains from the blacksmiths that led to it were not capped properly.
There were chapel outings as well as Sunday School outings.
The Kirks were involved in everything to do with the Chapel. They remember going to Ruth Kirk's wedding, and there being only lemonade to drink, as they were staunch Methodists.
The gated roads of The Ridgemere and Beeby Roads were remembered. There were four on the Beeby Road, and three on the Ridgemere. The first on the Ridgemere was in the first dip, the next at the top of the first rise, the third in the next dip. Children would go out on Sundays when they would open them for the occasional car for a penny. The best time was when the Church spire was struck by lightning, when many people came to see it.
Freda showed a book, her school prize for the neatest girl. Every day the children were inspected by Miss Burrell; their hands, faces

and handkerchief. Freda's handkerchief for inspection was up her sleeve, and the one for use was hidden elsewhere. Freda said that when she went cycling along the Ridgemere she always wore Wellington boots because the road was thick with cow manure. Miss Harrison, another teacher, lived in the Old School House. Nurse Black was the midwife. You were posh if you had her, because she used to live in for a fortnight.

Mrs.Henrietta Symonds

Headmistress 1943 –1959

Henrietta Symonds was born in a farm 'near the brook' in Rearsby, and as a young girl she lived in a farm her grandfather rented on the Queniborough Road, and at Main Street, South Croxton.

Prior to going for Teacher Training Mrs Symonds did some Pupil Teaching in a small school down Memory Lane by the side of St.Mark's Church in Leicester. She trained to become a teacher at St.Peter's College, Peterborough, a C.of E.Training College.

Having lived in Leicester for several years it was during the Second World War while Leicester was being bombed that she and her family moved to South Croxton.

She became the Headmistress of the school in 1943. She and her husband bought Sunny Dean, now called the Old School House. She taught alone in the school, with pupils aged 5 to 11 years old. Sometimes there were as many as 25 pupils in the school. She taught both her sons, Roy and Brian, until they left for Secondary schools. Roy transferred to the City Boys at the age of 10 instead of 11, a tribute to his mother's teaching. As a teacher she was fair but firm, and cared greatly for each of her pupils.

Although she taught all subjects, Art and Music were her two favourites. Occasionally the school was used for special events and concerts. During Mrs.Symonds' time as Headmistress school meals were cooked by her friend Mrs.Draycott, and later by Mrs.Ingram.

She was commended many times by the Managers of the school for her work, and particularly for the results she obtained in public examinations.

She dedicated her life to the school and her pupils, but unfortunately she died on December 23rd. 1959, aged 59 years,

After her death her husband, Harold Symonds, donated a silver cross and candlesticks to South Croxton Church in her memory.

Sylvia and Roy Symonds *(sadly, Roy died in 2007)*

Memories of an evacuee

In 1944, my mother and sister left Beckenham, Kent, where the V1 and V2 bombs were considered too dangerous, and came to live at the cottage in South Croxton which at that time was owned by my father's aunt, Mrs Teresa Stokes, who lived in Leicester. We believe that she had bought the cottage shortly before the war just for weekend use. My mother and sister stayed there for about 6 months or more; my father, who was still working in Beckenham, came to visit occasionally and I had previously been evacuated to Yorkshire. I was sent down to the cottage for the school summer holidays in 1944 at the age of 11, so I was probably there for about 5 or 6 weeks.

South Croxton was a very small village, but I recall little of it. When I visited it recently, I was surprised to find that the pub was on the corner of the lane - I thought I remembered it being further down the main road, but it seems unlikely that it has moved! The main reason for me to visit the village was to collect water from the iron pump in the yard of Kirk's Farm, opposite the end of the lane. This was the nearest source of water for the cottage and I used to carry it up the lane two bucketsful at a time. As the lane was just a rough, un-made-up track, this was quite a chore and we had to be very careful with our use of water. We became quite skilled in washing up and bathing in just a few cupfuls of it. On the rare occasions that we kids had a bath it was taken in a tin tub in the front garden.

There were a lot of American servicemen in the area in 1944. I always understood that they were based at an airfield at Syston, but cannot be sure of the location. We certainly used to talk about the Syston air base, but never knew anything about it. The GIs used to travel around in various vehicles, and would descend on the pub in considerable numbers. When my father visited, he would complain that the pub only had beer once a week (probably not true) and that the Americans grabbed it all! They certainly enjoyed visiting an Olde English Pub, even if it served warm beer. They also left an enormous amount of litter at the roadsides. I remember seeing masses of old paper, cigarette packets and other debris which had obviously been tossed out of a truck. We kids used to go through it in the hope, occasionally realised, of finding a few fags left in a pack, or other treasure. And if an American truck passed you, and you looked sufficiently appealing, they would always throw out a stick or two of chewing gum. By and large they were friendly folk and I don't think the locals resented them very much. I remember the awe with which my father recounted how the GIs drank with and addressed their officers by their first names, something that would never have happened in the British army.

The only child in the village I got to know was Ruth Kirk, the farmer's daughter. She was about my own age, around 12, so if she still survives she would be in her mid to late 70s. My sister knew other children, but cannot recall any names. A real highlight of our stay was the occasional trip to the bright lights of Leicester.

Not often, as there was just one bus a week to Leicester and one to Melton Mowbray. But we visited my Great-Aunt occasionally and had a real bath, electric light and proper cooked food.

As I have said, the lane up to the cottage was not made up, and as far as I can recall had no other houses in it. It was also unnamed, or at least we never knew it as anything but The Lane. There were just fields all the way up to the cottages, where the path stopped. Next to the cottage was a field with cows and a muddy pond into which we kids fell from time to time. The cottage (and I cannot recall it being called Fox Cottage at the time) was, and is, attached to another. This was occupied by a farm labourer named Jim Payne, who lived there alone. He was a taciturn man, never spoke unless absolutely necessary, and was out every day soon after dawn. One day, my mother came downstairs to find that he had left us a whole lot of freshly-picked mushrooms all laid out on the wall in front of the cottage. He continued to do this regularly while we were there. Perhaps he was just shy of these London Folk who had invaded his privacy.

The cottage itself was, of course primitive in the extreme. No drains, water, gas or electricity. Seeing it again recently, there were several features which I did not recognise. My sister seems to remember a lean-to on the right hand side, used for storage of some sort, but neither of us can recall any outbuildings of any kind. The land extended round the right-hand side, but we cannot recall any sort of back garden, nor a back door to the cottage. I am sure we would have remembered playing in it if there had been one. There was no front hedge, just a low stone wall. The privy was an earth closet in the garden at the side of the house. Inside, lighting was by oil lamp and all cooking was done on the open fire. There was a trivet for a kettle and an open-sided oven, like a biscuit tin on its side, into which we put meat and stood it in front of the fire to cook. It took hours! But I am sure I remember some sort of small cooker in the kitchen. Perhaps it was just a gas ring (bottled gas?) or a wood-fired hotplate device. It couldn't have had an oven or we would have used it instead of the fire. But we were eating very simple food, much of which didn't need cooking, and I certainly don't remember ever going hungry.

The stairs were in the corner of the living room and led up to I think two very small bedrooms. I do not remember the other door in the living room which is now the back door; perhaps this was a later addition. But the general layout of the ground floor is almost exactly as I remember it 64 years ago.

At the end of the summer holidays I returned to Yorkshire and my mother and sister stayed on at the cottage. But soon after, the bombing threat receded and we all came home. I don't know how much longer my aunt kept the cottage, or whether she ever used it after the war. But we always had happy memories of our stay in the country. My mother died in 2002 aged 91 and she often spoke of the days spent in South Croxton during the war. Primitive it may have been, but a good deal better than living in 'bomb alley' of the South-East.

Peter Reardon

South Croxton Remembered

My late father supplied newspapers to Rearsby, Gaddesby, Thorpe Satchville, Barsby, Ashby Folville and South Croxton. This was all started in the 1930s right through World War II and years after. As soon as I was old enough - about 14 - I used to help on Sundays. In fact I learned to drive all round the villages. During the war all the roads between the villages were lined with H.E (high explosive) bombs, the property of the American Air Force, who occupied many large properties - Gaddesby Hall, Ashby Pastures, etc.

My family all came from Cumberland before going to the USA. On their return they settled in Leicester. My father built the Rearsby garage. Then my grandparents came down. My uncle, Jim Stanton, worked at Auster Aircraft on Gaddesby Lane, and my auntie at Taylacraft at Thurmaston. Also I remember the spire at South Croxton being struck by lightning.

Stanton Bell (Sadly Stanton died in 2007)
Oadby

Fox Cottage - Home of a Child.

Here I stood admiring the front of Fox Cottage with two of my grandchildren at my feet. It was now the mid-1990's and I was experiencing an overwhelming feeling of nostalgia and excitement. I explained that this was the place I was born in 1933 as Freda Lockwood and spent the first six years of my life. Many years later I became Freda Mitchell when I got married.

The appearance of the cottage had changed dramatically since my time there but that wasn't surprising considering it was a run down red brick building in desperate need of a face lift. Despite this my time in the cottage was happy and my memories are filled with a safe and cosy warmth. Everyday seemed to be sunny and warm with hours spent in the garden among an abundance of flowers and trees. The road to the cottage (well I call it a road it was more like a cart track) was lined with high hedges stretching along either side. Only two cottages were present on the lane, ours and the adjoining home of Mr Payne.

Mr Payne lived next door with his mother, an elderly lady known simply as `Granny Payne'. Granny Payne never took kindly to cheeky youngsters like myself consequently earning me a stinging smack from mother. Mr Payne the farm worker always passed the time of day with my father, including the day this was done through our kitchen window while resting a spade on his shoulder, resulting in me chasing my brother and running into the spade, cutting my head so badly I still carry the scar to this day.

Moving back to the cottage itself we were lucky enough to meet the present owner who kindly invited me in for a look around what was once my home. This excited me and once inside I immediately noticed how much smaller it now seemed in comparison to my childhood days. The most prominent difference to me was the back door which we were never fortunate enough to have. The bathroom had also been moved inside where previously this was an outside wash house containing a fire copper and a large biscuit coloured sink. Mother always heated water in the copper and although designed for clothes washing we often got a wash ourselves when the sink could be used as a bath.

The water for this was from a well at the bottom of the garden, collected by lowering a bucket into the deep, cold water. The well was surrounded by brambles and covered with a wooden slatted top; this was to stop the obvious happening if we had attempted to climb on it. Everyday came with a threat from mother about not going near the well resulting in a deep fear being permanently rooted in all of us. Our toilet was also at the bottom of the garden. It was a moveable shed known as a `Soil Toilet' which constantly created a poignant stench meaning we willingly stayed away from that end of the garden and the dreaded well.

Speaking of fears another terrifying memory of mine was that of the hunt making its way up the lane. Being a small child faced with gigantic horses and baying hounds I often found refuge in what I thought was the safest place, behind mother's skirt!

Opposite the cottage was my idea of heaven at the time, a large meadow which in summertime was full of cowslips, buttercups and daisies. My sister and I spent many happy hours in there either running amongst the flowers or paddling in the tiny stream at the bottom.

The highlight of the village calendar was when the fair settled in the field behind the pub. Being only a young child I'm afraid my memories of this are vague and were prompted by my brother's recollections.

We all attended the tiny two roomed village school, except my sister who was too young at the time. I clearly remember the break time refreshments of warm Horlicks and biscuits. Due to us being poor and not having many toys much of our time at home was spent with a paper and pencil. This meant, thanks to my brother's teachings, I could answer simple sums by my second day at school much to the teacher's surprised delight. A kitchen table covered in newspaper instead of a tablecloth was studied at the silent mealtimes thus enabling me to vaguely pick up words from an early age.

The sad day arrived in the year of 1939 when we had to leave the cottage and move to a neighbouring village. Father had a new job as the head gardener in a hall in Thorpe Satchville. All our worldly goods were piled into a van, the family climbed in the back and the little cottage became a small dot in the distance. My life continued in Thorpe Satchville and then Leicester.

On reflection now I have revisited the village of South Croxton I feel the modern houses have replaced the small, pretty quaint village I remember. It's clear to me that South Croxton has been bought into the present day but my memories will always remain the same.

Freda Mitchell (née Lockwood)

View from the Church Tower

Timeline of South Croxton

500 – an historical event;
500 - beginning of a reign;
500 - event in the village

	B.C.	
Bronzed Age Begins	2500	Hodgkins claims that Bronze Age artefacts have been found along the Ridgemere and in the village
Iron Age begins	600	
Spread of Celts by infiltration and invasion	500	
	A.D.	
Full scale Roman Invasion	43	
Roman Conquest Complete	75	
Romans withdraw from Britain	407	
Saxon Invasions	500	

	800	This was probably the latest date by which a Saxon settlement was established here. The inhabitants had a place of worship on the site of the present Church.
Danelaw established	878	
	880	Earliest possible date by which Westhorpe was established on the edge of the village to the north. It was west of the Church.
Edward the Confessor	*1066*	
William invades England	1066	
William the Conqueror	*1066*	
	1068	Possible date of the Norman Church, and it and its furnishings were donated by Adulfus de Bruchi to replace the Preaching Cross

Domesday published	1087	
Henry !	*1100*	
Stephen	*1136*	
Matilda	*1141*	
Henry II	*1154*	
Richard the Lionheart	*1189*	
John	*1199*	
Henry 111	*1216*	
	1227	The Manor was given by Henry III to his Chief Justuice, Hubert de Burgh
Edward I	*1272*	
	1284	Dispute between the Priory of Malton and the nuns of Stamford at the Leicester Assizes over the ownership of land in the village
	1289	Suit between William Bassett, Rector of Ashby Folville, and William Burrell about the common pasture

	1300	Richard and Alice Asby held the manor Croxton Abbey paid a fee of 20 marks for a license to use half the land owned by the Church Malton Priory paid a fee of 5 marks entitling them to collect certain rents John Ashby held lands for Croxton Abbey Roger FitzRoger recovered an amount of land from John Cleaver
Edward II	*1307*	
	1314	The Manor and lands in the village were developed, and a new Church built – the present one
Edward III	*1327*	
	1344	Rectory charged two shillings for Peters Pence
	1346	Richard de Ashby was ‘lord of this village’. Edward of Woodstock, for knighting the King’s son, was linked with lands in the village

Richard III	*1377*	
Henry IV	*1399*	
Henry V	*1413*	
Battle of Agincourt	1415	
Henry VI	*1422*	
	1450	Approximate date of the adding of the south aisle and a new roof to the Church
	1452	Anthony Mallory was Lord of the Manor
		The moat behind the Church was dug within a few years of this date
Edward VI	*1461*	
Caxton's first printing press	1474	
Edward V	*1483*	
Henry VII	*1485*	
	1504	32 families in the village, about 144 people
Henry VIII	*1509*	
	1510	John Palmer 'a sound husbandman' (see Quotations)

	153?	Dom Thomas Eyre the last Catholic Priest
	153?	Thomas Ayle the first Church of England Minister
	1543	Thomas Manners, First Earl of Rutland, owner of many estates and former monasteries, a favourite of Henry VIII, bequeathed his lands in South Croxton
Beginning of Reformation	1536	
Edward VI	*1547*	
Jane	*1543*	
Mary	*1553*	
	1555	Eight shillings collected for the poor of the parish
Elizabeth I	*1558*	
	1564	There were 32 families in the village, about 144 people
	1575	The date noted of the death of Mary Barnes on her memorial in the Church

Spanish Armada	1588	
Cottage Industries	1600+	
James I	*1603*	
Charles I	*1625*	
	1630	Freeholders were William Goddard, gentleman, Thomas Allen, gentleman, Robert Veuly, constable, William Palmer
	1636	The bells of the Church were hung
	1640	First mention of Adcocks in the village
Civil War	1642	
Oliver Cromwell	*1649*	
	1655	The Rectory was charged two shillings for Peters Pence
Richard Cromwell	*1658*	
Charles II	*1660*	
James II	*1685*	
William III & Mary	*1689*	
Anne	*1702*	
George II	*1714*	

	1725	Fox Cottages built as labourers cottages for Baggrave Estate
George II	*1727*	
	1757	Nether Manor enclosed without Act of Parliament
	1770	The King family came and farmed in the village
	1773	Date noted on the memorial slab in the South Aisle of the death of Mary Pick
		There were 100 dwellings in the village and 20 freeholders
William IV	*1830*	
Victoria	*1837*	
	1866	Triple Cottage (83/85/87) built
	1867	Primitive Methodist Chapel built in Kings Lane, renamed Chapel Lane

	1881	The Black family moved into the village. In 2007 Frank was farming at Gothic Farm, one of three left in the village. In 1951 there were 10.
	1884	School built and opened. 340 villagers, 13 trades followed
	1889	Considerable work done on the Church windows and tower
Edward VII	*1901*	
George V	*1910*	
First World War	1914-18	Territorial Army hut built in School Lane. Later becoming the Village Hall
	1921	Lance-Corporal Weldon killed in N.Ireland
	1925	A major reconstruction of the Church.The North wall had separated from the tower and the wall bowed outwards, and the rest was in an unsatisfactory condition
	1932	Electricity came to the village
Edward VIII	*1936*	
George VI	*1936*	

	1936	Church tower struck by lightening
		Electric heating and lighting first installed in the Church by Bob Parkinson
Second World War	*1939-45*	
	1941	The Symonds moved into the Old School House
		Mr.& MrsKirk left Maida Vale Farm, bringing to an end 200 years in which that family had farmed
	1947	The blacksmiths was incorporated into the Golden Fleece
	1951	Methodist Chapel in School Lane demolished. Lane reverted to Kings Lane
Elizabeth II	*1952*	
	1952	Mains water came to the village
	1956	Freda and Fred Elliott became landlords of the Golden Fleece
	1957	Long article in The Advertiser. July 13th.
	1962	Do-it-yourself floodlighting to the Church

1964	May 30th. Village Fête opened by Ted Moult, a TV personality, to raise funds for the Village Hall
1966	Village had its first telephones and main sewerage
1969	Marion Aldis opened the Pottery
1970	Church bells taken down and placed on a platform in the Tower
1972	The village bought the school and playground from Leicestershire County Council for £8,500 to be used as a Village Hall
	Maida House Farm was demolished
1973	The official opening of the 'new' Village Hall 30th May
1974	The first Arts Festival, organised by John Refern and family. It became a biennial event after 1978, missing only 1980. In 1982 it

1974	resumed with a committee helping him, until 2002.
	Mediaeval coin found in Rectory Gardens
	New Rectory built
1977	‘Dr.Who’, written by Marion Aldis, was performed in the Village Hall
1978	New Rectory built
1984	Freda and Fred Elliott retired from the Golden Fleece
1989	Parish Council was formed
	July – first edition of The Clarion
1991	Clarion reported that a seat in the churchyard dedicated to the memory of Mrs.Una Clarke had been stolen and a tombstone smashed
1993	A gas supply was piped into the village from the North Sea pipeline which ran along the Queniborough Road
1995	Start of the Church Planned Giving
1997	A Village Appraisal Committee was set up

2000	Refurbishment of the Church floodlightighng in time for the Millennium
	December – last edition (so far) of The Clarion Village History and Walks published in the village
2001	Proposal made to purchase the Village Hall playing field
	Last Arts Festival held
2004	Internet Broadband came to the village: there was still little mobile phone reception in the village
2005	May – the Village website – www.south-croxton.org.uk was established
2005	June – the Golden Jubillee obelisk was unveiled
	October - this book was completed
2007	This book and an accompanying disc was published

About the author.....

Philip Snelders has been in education all his life. From teaching in Primary and Secondary schools, he went into Teacher Training, first at Borough Road College in London, then in Leicester at Scraptoft when it was the City of Leicester Teacher Training College. It then became the Leicester College of Education, then part of the Leicester Polytechnic, and finally part of De Montfort University. He was the B.Ed.Tutor, the Co-ordinator of Education Studies, and finally Deputy Head of the School of Education. He was made redundant in 1985, and taught part time in four Midlands Universities, and then as a supply teacher in Primary and Secondary schools. In his seventies he still goes into Gaddedesby school each week to teach as a volunteer because he misses teaching and children. He is the author of a book on Gregorian Chant, co-editor of a series of 10 books in Philosophy of Education which he devised, and author of articles, papers, and book reviews in Philosophy of Education and in Curriculum Studies. He added to his academic achievements by getting a GCSE in Archaeology at the age of 71yrs. He came to the village in 1980, served on the Parish Council for eight years, and the South Croxton Arts Festival committee for twelve years where he was organiser of the musical and other events. His proudest achievement are his children, Susan, David and Michael and five grandchildren, Chris, Jenny, Joshua Philip, Sam, and Nicki, his two step-children Gavin and Justine and four step-grandchildren, Molly, Edward, Daniel and Daisy, who are often seen filling the house in the village leaving his wife Lesley and himself delighted but exhausted. He is grateful to his wife for this and many things, but particularly for putting up with his enthusiasm for the past.

Index